Tough Talks
Navigating Through the Marital Rough Spots

DR. JOE STEWART

Copyright © 2026 by Dr. Joe Stewart

All rights reserved. No portion of this publication may be reproduced, stored in an electronic system, or transmitted in any form by any means, electronic, mechanical, photocopy, recording, or otherwise, without the author's prior permission, except with brief quotations used in literary reviews and specific non-commercial uses permitted by copyright law. Please use the contact information at the back of this book for permission requests.

The views expressed in this book are the author's and do not necessarily reflect those of the publisher.

-Scripture references marked as "NIV" are taken from the Holy Bible, New International Version®, NIV® Copyright ©1973, 1978, 1984, 2011 by Biblica, Inc.® Used by permission. All rights reserved worldwide.
-Scripture references marked as "ESV" are taken from The Holy Bible, English Standard Version. ESV® Text Edition: 2016. Copyright © 2001 by Crossway Bibles, a publishing ministry of Good News Publishers. All rights reserved.
-Scripture references marked as "NLT" are taken from the Holy Bible, New Living Translation, Copyright © 1996, 2004, 2015 by Tyndale House Foundation. Used by permission of Tyndale House Publishers, Inc., Carol Stream, Illinois 60588. All rights reserved.
-Scripture references marked as "NKJV" are taken from the New King James Version®. Copyright © 1982 by Thomas Nelson. Used by permission. All rights reserved.
-Scripture references marked as "KJV" are taken from the King James Version (public domain).
-Scripture references marked "MSG" are taken from *THE MESSAGE*, Copyright © 1993, 2002, 2018 by Eugene H. Peterson. Used by permission of NavPress. All rights reserved. Represented by Tyndale House Publishers, Inc.
-Scripture references marked as "PHILLIPS" are taken from The New Testament in Modern English by J.B. Phillips, Copyright © 1960, 1972 J.B. Phillips. Administered by The Archbishops' Council of the Church of England. Used by Permission.

Cover and Interior Layout by 2026 Harvest Creek Publishing and Design www.harvestcreek.net.

Ordering information: Churches, associations, and others may obtain information about quantity purchases by emailing info@harvestcreek.net.

Tough Talks—1st ed.
ISBN: 978-1-961641-44-0

Printed in the United States of America

Praise For This Book

A real marriage isn't perfect. A real marriage is two people being perfected, and the rough spots we all experience in marriage are the very things that God uses to shape, mold, form, and perfect us to become more like Jesus. Dr. Joe Stewart explores this reality on the pages of this book. As a pastor, he brings strong spiritual teaching, and as a husband, he brings real-life, practical advice. If you're married, you need this book!

Mark and Jill Savage
Co-authors of the book, *No More Perfect Marriage*
Co-hosts of the *No More Perfect* Podcast at *www.MarkandJill.org*
Check out their "Marriage 2.0 Intensive Retreat" at
https://jillsavage.org/hope-renewed-intensive-retreat/

Dr. Joe Stewart has long been a faithful preacher of God's Word, and now he brings that same wisdom and clarity to the written page. *Tough Talks: Navigating Through the Marital Rough Spots* is both practical and deeply biblical, offering couples real tools for walking through conflict with honesty, grace, and hope. With warmth and candor, Dr. Stewart reminds us that differences don't have to divide but can be opportunities for growth and deeper intimacy when handled with love and truth. His stories, insights, and step-by-step guidance will encourage couples to see marriage not as a burden but as a God-given partnership that reflects His design. This book is a much-needed resource for anyone longing to strengthen their marriage and navigate the rough spots with courage and faith.

Aurora de Rodriguez, PhD
Academia GCN Executive Director *Tough*

Tough Talks is a powerful and truthful guide for anyone seeking a godly marriage. It does not offer quick fixes or empty encouragement. Instead, Joe weaves Scripture and practical wisdom together, showing how God uses our differences to shape us and strengthen our relationships. I found myself laughing and nodding throughout, recognizing my marriage in the stories he shared. These moments reminded me that laughter, patience, and a generous dose of grace are what carry a marriage through its quirks and challenges. *Tough Talks i*s a beautiful reminder that love is not simply a feeling, but a commitment built on patience, humility, and daily effort. We are proud of Joe for writing such a heartfelt and insightful book. It is a light for couples who want to grow closer through faith, understanding, and perseverance.

Miguel Carnero
Deacon First Baptist Church Seminole

I have known Joe Stewart since our junior high school days. He is my friend and is now my pastor. He has a great ability for leadership and dedicates his life to Kingdom work. He is especially gifted, along with his wife, Nancy, to equip married couples through marital ups and downs. Joe works hard to strengthen the family bonds, as seen in his first book, *Love Handles.* Now, in the latest book *Tough Talks,* he looks for ways to facilitate conflict resolution through biblical wisdom and Christian values.

David Stone
Deacon Chairman of FBC Seminole

Contents

Praise For This Book 3

Contents 5

Dedication 7

Acknowledgments 9

Foreword 11

Introduction 13

Chapter 1 - Differences and Distance 17

Chapter 2 - Differences Are Not Deficiencies 28

Chapter 3 - Start-Ups and Clutches 45

Chapter 4 - Hellos and Goodbyes 58

Chapter 5 - Recipes and Roots 77

Chapter 6 - Apologies and Mirrors 93

Chapter 7 - Forgiveness and Referees 108

Chapter 8 - Hard Talks and Carry-Ons 129

Chapter 9 - Aisle Seats and Runways 146

Chapter 10 - Marriage: The Power of Us 162

About the Author 168

Dedication

*To my wife, Nancy Thornhill Stewart,
45 down and forever to go.*

Acknowledgments

I am indebted to many people for the book you presently view. I'm thankful on the heavenly side to **Mom and Dad.** Someday we'll share a cup of Joe, and we can talk about this together. I'll also hug **Delwin and Thelma Thornhill** and thank them for the great gift given in my wife.

I'm also thankful to **Margie Emig**, my admin at FBC, for her initial honing of my work. I appreciate my friend, **John Hogan,** for giving it a go as well. I'm grateful to **Teresa Granberry** and her team for giving such faithful support. Great kudos to **Sherman and Tammy Aten** and **Three2One Ministries,** for your partnership in the gospel. I also appreciate my three daughters for the seven grandsons they have allowed us the pleasure of spoiling. Thanks, **Pamela, Kimberly, and Kristen,** for your loving support. I am also grateful to the **entire FBC staff and church** for your prayers, partnership, support, and encouragement.

Thank you most of all to **Jesus** for making beauty out of brokenness. You are the pearl of great price.

Finally, thanks to **you, the reader**, for trusting me with your time and allowing me to share my words and life with you. What a gift.

Foreword

What a most humbling privilege it is to write this foreword for our lifelong friends, Dr. Joe and Nancy Stewart. This is the couple God placed in our lives at the beginning of our marriage, who quickly became our first "couple friends". I would hope you all have *that* couple! If so, it would do you well to nourish this one-of-a-kind relationship. It becomes sweeter year after year. Anytime you can vacation with another couple, and still like each other afterwards? Well, you'd better hold on to them!

The Stewarts are not only friends but also play an integral part on our ministry's Board of Directors. They serve with us at home and abroad as staff of Three2One Marriage Conferences. What a perfect teaching team they make. They are also co-contributors for our book, *Touching Base*. And now their second marriage book is here, *Tough Talks*.

What makes this book fun for us is that we can vouch for many of these stories personally! We were in Spain in Chapter 3! And we have laughed and cried over many of their marriage melee . . . after the fact, of course. It's the best entertainment and counseling! And it's FREE!

Now, *Tough Talks*. You have picked up a book that will:

- Make you smile with the "I can relate to that!"
- Exclaim "Ahaa!" to a story that just taught you something, or
- Make you giggle about something that will soon feel like a smashing of the toes!

It is loaded with teaching based on Bible principles that are proven in the marriage of Joe and Nancy. And if that was all it was, you could become the smartest couple in the room. But you will soon see a genuine couple walking through raw issues on a beautiful but "not without trauma" journey, and it highlights almost every marital issue common to man and wife.

One of the greatest truths shared is this: Couples start off trying to change their spouse right after the recession! Joe and Nancy show that both need some sanding, and God has prepared the custom grade sandpaper for you—in your spouse. So, the next time you are waylaid by just how different your spouse is, hold thy tongue and remind yourself, "God fashioned [Fill in the blank] just for me!"

Few couples are willing to share their painful, sometimes embarrassing, and vulnerable moments with the world, but that is the heart of this book, and they have done it so well. You may feel you are sitting in their kitchen or bedroom! Joe's detailed expressions of his own marriage, his quips and her quips, coupled with Biblical wisdom, make this a book we encourage married/engaged couples of all ages to get their hands on.

We all have tough talks, no matter how long we've been on the marriage road. They don't stop, because we never fully "arrive" down here. We still need help to navigate what is about to come around the corner. Here is a trustworthy marriage compass for you both. Prepare to take off!

Thank you, Stews!

Sherman & Tammy Aten
Founders of Three2One Marriage & authors of
Touching Base: A Couple's Devotional

Introduction

Isn't it funny how quickly wardrobes change once you get married? Date night pre-marriage included dressing up and paying immense attention to the details of the overall look. Down the road, in a few years, what you wear shifts. Instead of chiffon, it's flannel, flannel, Walmart T-shirts, and anything comfortable. There's something about adding kids to the equation, pets peeing on the carpet, and multiple transitions that change the vibe in your marriage.

I'd be lying to say our married life has always been long runways and smooth landings. There has been a lot of turbulence, missed connections, and long layovers in uncomfortable settings. We love each other deeply, but when our kids create chaos, jobs bring stress, and personalities clash, sometimes we don't really like each other very much. We have learned we are opposites in almost every area. She's a homebody. I'm on the go. She likes the cold and mountains. I like the beach and HOT weather. She's laid back. I'm not. You get the picture. Someone has said, "Opposites attract, and then they attack."

The truth is, early in our marriage, we fought on the days that ended in "Y." It wasn't always small skirmishes, but as one married couple said, "it was middle school drama-level melees." Knock-down, drag-outs, rock-'em sock-'em robots stuff. It's not the image a pastor likes to present on Sunday mornings, but it was a behind-the-scenes reality. We fought about everything: money, in-laws, sex, kids, pets, underwear, swimwear, work schedules, chores, who's going to the store, and a host of other things. We've had lots of practice doing conflict in unhealthy ways and with rough landings. So, we decided to try different approaches to boarding, takeoff, and landing difficult conversations, including putting in the work with counselors, marriage workshops, and biblical strategies to find a path to smoother touchdowns.

No one wants to board a Boeing 737 that loses a door plug and rips away clothing, allowing cell phones to be hurled through a gaping hole in the fuselage. An investigation of the Alaska Airlines flight that took off from Portland, Oregon, discovered that the plane had left the factory missing the four bolts needed to hold the door in place. Even at the beginning, when a marriage is shiny and new, and everything looks and smells good, there are missing pieces. After a while and a bit of miles down the road, even the best marriages have issues that need maintenance. Instead, many couples sweep the hard stuff under the rug and keep on taxiing down the runway.

Taxiing without addressing the taxing issues will eventually create real fissures. Intimacy will crater, personalities will clash, and often, when real differences aren't discussed, the marriage is totaled. Nobody says vows on a wedding day, anticipating such a wreck at the end. It's why we constantly say awkward conversations are better than avoidance. Also, to remind you, falling in love is easy, but staying in love requires a plan.

That's the intention of this book. It's intended to help you continually fall in love with the one you fell in love with. It's not in-depth counseling for those teetering on the cliff of marital collapse, but it is helpful for those married spouses who are dealing with daily irritations and want to feel heard and seen. This book gives seat assignments for married couples to practice as they begin tough talks that become useful conversations. It's moving the marriage towards smoother takeoffs and easier landings by addressing genuine issues, such as:

- How to deal with hidden issues
- Realizing differences aren't deficiencies

- Learning the best start-ups
- Rituals and routines of hellos and goodbyes
- Amending your secret contracts
- Learning to be holy and live peaceably
- Crafting genuine apologies
- Climbing the ladder of forgiveness
- Prepping for a hard talk
- Asking for what you want
- Landing on the runway to a better relationship

The intent is to arrive at the destination you signed up for—a healthy marriage. It's not to paint a picture of the false front of the Stepford wives. Marriage is hard. Marriage requires work. It's two different people with conflicting sets of expectations and varying personalities trying to sync up and mesh together. Marriage is messy and includes navigating how to discover your mate is done for the day once the bra is off and the jammies are on.

Conflict resolution in marriage means learning to de-escalate instead of escalating the emotions and causing a meltdown. Too many couples leave the runway and bail from the airport, refusing to work through the issues at hand. The intent of this work is to help you learn to stay in the airport and stay on the runway of the current conversation. You'll learn to break down where things broke down, and you will eventually find a rhythm that works for you.

You will learn that you can always be right and never be reconciled, or you can surrender your right to be right and find reunion. Actual progress is made towards lifting your relationship off the runway when you listen to understand rather than listen to defend. You will learn to draw close by just saying, "Yeah, that really sucks. I'm super sorry." Too often, we would rather say, "Suck it up, buttercup." A quick aside from personal experience: that lights everything on fire.

Rather than run for the exits, you learn to sit in the middle of the suck. Usually, the awkwardness lasts for about as long as a seven-second smooch. It's not nearly as pleasant, but in the end, it might lead to longer times of canoodling.

So, buckle up and get in your seat. You are in for some turbulence as you take off on the journey to relearn how to tackle tough talks. You will learn that sometimes fighting in your marriage is fighting for your marriage. You will discover a simple tool that makes a huge difference: no matter how long you've been married, you must ask for what you want. We aren't mind readers, and your spouse will not be able to know what you want without you asking. See? That alone is worth the price of the book!

No one knows what you want unless you ask them. Try it. Don't be subtle. Don't be suggestive. Don't be indirect. Look your partner in the eyes and hit your partner up for exactly what you need.

The goal isn't a perfect relationship and a marriage report card with straight A's and zero demerits. Instead, aim for solid B's and eliminate putting things off, keeping things hidden, and pretending everything is hunky-dory. Remember! You aren't in this alone. God is fighting with you and for you. He's in it for the long haul.

Chapter 1

Differences and Distance

Many of us experiment with filters on our Instagram feeds. Some filters are fun and playful and allow couples to swap faces and wear fuzzy ears. The personal filters quickly make anyone look better and younger. The apps fine-tune faces to hide the flaws and accentuate what is attractive, including smoother skin, fuller lips, and pointy noses.

The reality of marriage is that you see the other person, filter-free. Every imperfection is magnified, and every struggle is amplified. Roles and preferences uncover differences inherited from family dynamics. Marriage exposes disagreements that occur when neither party is right nor wrong.

For example, years ago, in our backyard, I loved the creativity and autonomy of our daughters jumping on the trampoline from the top of the shed. Goodness, my daughters even invited the neighbors to join in the fun.

My wife, Nancy, expected broken arms and lawsuits in her quest for security and sanctuary. My suggestion that Nancy "lighten up" failed to resolve the problem. Neither did her accessing her mental file to highlight several friends who bought into her side of things.

In his book, *The Seven Principles for Making Marriage Work*, psychologist John Gottman labels this merry-go-round of differences as perpetual problems that are never resolved. They make up almost seventy percent of the conflict in every marriage. These recurring issues run the gamut from how to load the dishwasher (knives down and forks up) to when to arrive for a party (ten minutes early is late).

Even the need to use a digital password organizer (absolutely) can create conflict. A nationwide survey of perceptive people generated answers for this assessment. Anyway, I'm only asking for a friend.

Even though we see our mate with all their foibles and flaws, we still maintain several lenses through which we look at life. And these lenses color our perspective. Milan and Kay Yerkovich, in their book *How We Love: Discover Your Love Style, Enhance Your Marriage*, describe in detail the distinctive viewpoints between a man and a woman. These viewpoints include:

- Life experiences
- Home environments
- Gender differences
- Personality wirings
- Love styles
- Unspoken rules (i.e., birthdays are big deals)
- Love languages
- How much planning we prefer

These innate profiles can create frustration (like when I leave a pile on my nightstand). Or they can create fascination (like when Nancy writes detailed lists for her to-do countdown). How we interpret the world through the lenses we use is not an inadequacy but a reality.

My family gives me a hard time about my eyeglasses constantly being covered with smudges. I rarely notice until I remove my spectacles and inspect them closely. 1 Corinthians 13:11-12 refers to our seeing through a mirror dimly. We must recognize the dimmed and blurred lenses through which we look at our mates. Thus, we will empathize better with our spouses' approach to navigating various issues. It's one way love grows us as maturity puts away childish attitudes and embraces growing up in loving our mate. Our way is not the only way or necessarily the right way. Accepting our nuances helps us close the distance. It allows our spouse to flourish as the fearfully and wonderfully made masterpiece God created him or her to be.

> When I was a child, I spoke like a child,
> I thought like a child, I reasoned like a child.
> When I became a man, I gave up childish ways.
> For now we see in a mirror dimly, but then face to face.
> Now I know in part; then I shall know fully,
> even as I have been fully known.
> 1 CORINTHIANS 13:11-12 ESV

SLOW FADES AND HIDDEN ISSUES

When rightly applied, marriage is one tool that prevents self-deception from walking in darkness and enables us to bring authentic confession to God. He is "faithful and just and will forgive us our sins and purify us from all unrighteousness" (1 John 1:8-9b [NIV]). As a matter of fact, this whole passage speaks of freedom for the married couple.

The difficulty in marriage comes when one partner doesn't acknowledge that personal filters exist. These filters color their viewpoints and can lead to self-sabotage. Professing innocence and refusing to acknowledge difficulties means truth is absent, and darkness clouds our vision. Relational harmony (fellowship with one another) occurs only when we allow light to shine and bring clarity. Hiding in the darkness leads to dishonesty and relational distance.

In his book *A Lasting Promise: A Christian Guide to Fighting for Your Marriage,* marital researcher Scott Stanley offers valuable insights. He calls these mental filters about how life is supposed to look and feel "hidden issues." He explains that these hidden issues can "fester and produce fear, sadness, and resentment that can erode and eventually destroy the marriage." Hidden issues must be brought to the surface.

When we ignore hidden issues of the heart, they will eventually bubble up as criticism, defensiveness, stonewalling, and contempt. John Gottman refers to these four behaviors in his book, *Why Marriages Succeed or Fail: And How You Can Make Yours Last.* He calls these behaviors the four horsemen of the apocalypse that lead a couple away from intimacy towards isolation. Jesus says in Mark 7:20 (NIV), "What comes out of a person is what defiles them." Unexamined inner attitudes hidden within breed distance.

In their book *No More Perfect Marriage,* Mark and Jill Savage identify seven ways differences can lead to slow fades. These slow fades happen in the little things simmering under the surface, in places and spaces unnoticed. These slow fades include unrealistic expectations, minimizing feelings and concerns, not accepting differences, disagreements, defensive responses, naivete, and avoiding emotions.

Relationships wither when the time and energy we put into our marriage are neglected, and we are disconnected. Life speeds up, attention slows down, and deposits in the marriage are missed. Marriages don't thrive in neutral or reverse. Small deposits made consistently over long periods of time bring compound interest.

Marriage must be maintained. Consider the analogy of a new car purchase that Paul David Tripp makes in his book, *Marriage: 6 Gospel Commitments Every Couple Needs to Make.* When we purchase a new car, we baby it. We follow scheduled maintenance and pay attention to recalls and service reminders.

It's not a hassle because we realize investments need constant care. We buy gadgets, cleansers, and deodorizers to keep things fresh and clean. We are attuned to weird noises when something isn't right.

However, at some point, our car is no longer new. It doesn't feel new since you spilled a Route 44 cherry Coke from Sonic on the way to work. When you drive your car, the engine makes sounds that didn't occur when it was new. And besides, we seem to have gotten a whole lot busier since we bought the car.

Finding time to keep it clean and change the oil is not as easy as it once was. At some point, it doesn't bother us that a week's worth of trash populates the floorboards and the back seats. We begin to let go of the good habits of auto care, and our car pays the price.

One morning, quite unexpectedly, we go to start our car, the oil light comes on, and the car won't start. We say, "Stupid car." But no. It should be "Stupid us." We should not be surprised that something is wrong, as we quit paying attention months ago. We forsook the habits that would have kept our car in good repair.

The character of a marriage is not formed in one grand moment. Relationships don't go bad in a marriage in an instant. Marriage goes bad progressively. The development and deepening of love in marriage happen through tasks that are done daily; this is also true with the sad deterioration of a marriage. The problem is that we simply don't pay attention and allow ourselves to think, desire, say, and "do life" in ways we shouldn't. We are irritated and exasperated. We allow petty stuff to accumulate.

We quit asking for forgiveness in moments of wrong. We complain about how the other does stuff and keep a record of wrongs, which blooms into irritation instead of appreciation. We neglect honing the brief moments, and they become bitter. The minor battles bloom into benign neglect and passivity. Sweetness evaporates. Friendship dissipates. They are replaced by distance, coldness, impatience, conflict, and irritation.

Sexual intimacy disappears. Sex isn't the fuel of a good relationship, by the way; it's the expression of one. If our relationships aren't daily acts of love, there is little chance that sex will be. Inattention to your mate allows your differences to create distance, and distance gives the devil an opportunity to keep widening the gap (Ephesians 4:26-27).

BLOOD IN THE WATER

Once, when we were vacationing in Key West, we splurged on a shark excursion. The crew poured ripped fish into the water, explaining that the blood would draw the sharks near the boat. Immediately, the sharks appeared behind the bow and feasted on the fish. We took photos, fascinated to be near something so dangerous.

This is how the Enemy works. He is drawn to blood. When the devil sees a marriage breaking down, he attacks because he sees blood in the water. Satan doesn't leave us alone when we are bleeding; he gains energy. The Evil One sees a chance for possible destruction. Injury—whether physical, relational, emotional, or spiritual—attracts him. It gives him an entry and an opportunity.

Our takeaway should be: Don't invite a shark to dinner! So why do many of us end up doing just that? By thinking we have arrived and letting go of good habits, we allow our differences to divide us rather than strengthen us. The Enemy knows when there is blood in the water. He enjoys nothing better than watching us bite and devour one another (Galatians 5:15) instead of serving one another humbly in love.

Neglecting our spouse is an invitation to the devil to do his worst. The devil sees the churn in the water and goes to work. He fills the gaps with hostility instead of serenity and indifference instead of intimacy. Satan is an adversary with a cunning strategy to lead us astray from walking with Jesus, which then separates our walk with one another.

In contrast, there is no greater heavenly sandpaper that God will use to make each of us more like Him than our spouses' innate and distinct personalities and proclivities. I know we'd prefer that life be easier, because this is a hassle. But God sees it as a holy way to craft us into the image of His Son. God fashioned our mates and declared His creation "good." We denigrate our spouses and decline to celebrate God's creative bent when we refuse to receive our mates as God's gracious gift. Rather than depreciating our mates, ask God to give us the ability to appreciate their gifts and personalities and celebrate the goodness of God.

We soon discover that knuckling down to sharpen our marriage skills is less effective than recognizing that, over the long haul, God uses our marriage to refine our own souls. Too often, when we hit a rough spot in our relationship, we go "all in," trying to bring about growth and change. We click on our Audible selections, go to coffee with a friend, casually mention a glaring issue to a mentor, or subscribe to some marriage guru. Then, when the rough spots remain, we are ready to throw in the towel. We fail to realize that genuine change is a process rather than an event that must marinate in the crevices of our marriage over a lengthy period.

What do we do? We should recognize that genuine change doesn't occur suddenly or immediately through grand gestures. The marriage works on you before you work on the marriage. Grand gestures are not nearly as effective as small gains. These gains can include holding our tongues when we want to unload, giving grace when we would rather save face, and initiating a hard conversation rather than retreating into isolation. These are all small steps that might bring an immediate return on investment or might yield near-zero results.

Just don't quit! Incremental. Intentional. We aren't on this journey for a quick trip. We are invested for the long haul—for the rest of our lives. Galatians 6:9 is instructive:

> Let us not become weary in doing good,
> for at the proper time
> we will reap a harvest if we do not give up.
> GALATIANS 6:9 NIV

We do not determine the proper time; that's God's business and a matter of His sovereignty. Spouses trust the process, even when problems persist. It takes two characteristics that the Proverbs mention repeatedly: diligence and prudence. Diligence continues, and prudence tells us where to invest. Inconsistency doesn't breed connection. Inconsistency brings defections.

SINGING MARITAL DUETS

I'm not much of a vocalist, but I sang a musical duet with Nancy at our wedding. She sings like Carrie Underwood, and I croon like Kermit the Frog. Singing is her lane. She flourishes in that arena.

Conversely, I know she isn't designed to juggle many balls simultaneously. At the same time, I can keep adding to my plate and flourish. She needs downtime, and I need constant action. Our capacities are not liabilities but varieties that bring opportunities. So, if we aren't perceiving how we are built differently, we wonder why our partner isn't cut from the same cloth as us.

We've adjusted and adapted to allow each other room to be our best selves. Others may not get it, but we *get* each other. There's now more living, forgiving, and seeing the best in our partner. I might even burst into song. In. The. Shower!

Too often, differences cause resentment because our spouse *isn't like us*. We need to learn that good duets warm up before the performance. They sing the scales to anticipate the wrong notes before they happen. Rehearsing your part before belting out a terrible performance with your mate is one path to dealing with hidden issues.

The raw reality is that marriage brings us face to face with our biggest marriage problem: ME! I am the one singing off-key. I'm not always in tune with my partner because my playlists are self-constructed to reflect the notes I want to underscore. Asking my spouse to sing the same note doesn't produce harmony or intimacy, but the noise of a clanging chorus. Blaming, shaming, withdrawing, stonewalling, criticizing, and a peace that is no peace prevent us from singing from the same sheet music.

Our Composer allows our differences to bring a better marital blend than singing solo. However, embracing that role requires remarkable humility. Particularly when we allow our partner to nudge us to sing more in tune with the notes God hopes we would use to sing in harmony. God wants to use our differences to create a better marriage with the partner we already have. Too often, our differences create "music" from our mate that we consider off-key. But the truth is, living with someone in perpetual close contact forces the hidden notes to surface and produce a better composition.

Beautiful music does not happen accidentally but interdependently. Louis K. Anspacher explained it well in the following quote:

> Marriage is that relation between a man and a woman
> in which the independence is equal,
> the dependence is mutual, and the obligations reciprocal.
> Louis K. Anspacher

God created marriage as the most important human relationship. He wants others to hear beautiful music played in our marriage and cause a watching world to want to sing along. Singing from the same sheet music means neither disengagement from our spouses nor enmeshment with our spouses. I'm not very good at singing harmony because I too often join Nancy on her part. That's not a duet. That's tone-deaf.

We must vocalize our own tunes in full and satisfying lives, so we are better together. Individuality and dignity are like two separate strings playing together on the same guitar from the same score. When either string is missing, the chorus crashes.

As marriages dissipate and disintegrate, couples often become roommates instead of lovers, singing from different scores. Such a state is a sad song. I'm currently listening to Captain and Tennille in the background; their marital journey was one of two soloists living together in emotional emptiness.

In her memoir, *Toni Tennille: A Memoir,* she describes a chronicle of the constant upheaval created by a protest polka of distance and pursuit. She pursued, and he rarely engaged except during performances on stage. Many couples follow this pattern of public relational harmony and private disconnection. The music many marriages play for public consumption is rarely replayed behind closed doors.

God created marriage for one-flesh intimacy, not disengaged disharmony. Marital duets are designed to fill gaps that decrease isolation and increase celebration. Do you remember Rocky Balboa's romantic declaration? "She's got gaps, I've got gaps, together we fill gaps." Gap-fillers need substance as they complement rather than complete one another. Such a mindset keeps the marriage in tune, reminding each partner how they auditioned each other to sing a lifetime duet.

A duet requires two individuals to show up and pay attention to the lives they are leading. If your voice is missing in the marriage, take responsibility and find your part to be a secure and solid self in the marriage. Two different individuals, owning their unique voices, maturely asking each other what they want, bring a marital duet worth hearing. Romans 15:5-6 (NIV) says:

> May the God who gives endurance and encouragement
> give you the same attitude of mind
> toward each other that Christ Jesus had,
> so that with one mind and one voice
> you may glorify the God and Father
> of our Lord Jesus Christ.
> ROMANS 15:5-6 NIV

Chapter 2

Differences Are Not Deficiencies

Nancy and I have been married 45 years and still discover differences in our DNA. I'm spontaneous and prefer activity. She's predictable and meticulous. I'm mercurial and often volatile. Nancy has an amazing capacity to gift wrap presents. They are packaged up tighter than Fort Knox and look like they belong on the cover of Architectural Digest.

It may seem silly, but this characteristic sometimes gets on my last nerve. I could not care less about what wrapping paper the gift comes in. I just want the present—give me the prize now! Airtight gift-wrapping only complicates getting to the goodies. Let's dispense with the tape and ribbons, put the present in a decorative sack, and call it good. I mean, my wife is a gift to me, and I want to unwrap her as fast as possible. *Wink. Wink.*

There are other ways we differ. Most often, I'm the initiator in our relationship, and she's the responder. It used to annoy and frustrate me. Now, I realize God built us this way. Despite not starting with the best dating game, I've elevated my romantic pursuits. I plan extravagant dates and elegant meals. I scour the internet for creative ways to show my love. I even named a star after my wife. Come on! Isn't that the best? In the vast universe, there's a supernova in a constellation named after my wife. I've got the certificate that cost me $39.99. It's such a sweeping gesture.

Her reaction was to sing Shania Twain's tune, "That Don't Impress Me Much." She'd rather that I do something practical, like vacuum or unclog the toilet. She calls it "chore play." Neither approach is wrong. Both are part of the endless varieties of how God hand-wraps human personalities. We are never identical. We are atypical.

The goal isn't to be the same. The goal is to be together. God's goal isn't uniformity; His goal is unity and intimacy. This reinforces the concept God uses in His discussion of various spiritual gifts. First Corinthians 12:6 (NLT) says, "God works in different ways, but it is the same God who does the work in all of us." That's obvious. God loves variety; He loves differences. God designs and refines your spouse so that their differences and viewpoints will create variety and discomfort. Variety is to be celebrated, and discomfort is to be embraced as a tool for God to craft you in His image.

We desire the unity of one flesh, but we are not the same. The dissimilarities can create distance. Distance that separates and isolates can lead to frustration instead of fascination, as noted in Mark and Jill Savage's book *No More Perfect Marriages: Experience the Freedom of Being Real Together*. When differences are seen as deficiencies, they can lead to a lack of decency as we begin to deplore what we should cherish. Satan's scheme from the beginning was to disrupt and interrupt what God labeled very good. He organizes a host of forces to attack intimacy and unity. He knows chaos ensues if he can divide and conquer the marriage team (Ephesians 6:12). Instead of going toe to toe with the Enemy, we concentrate our energies on our spouse as the enemy. Rather than fighting for one another, we fight with one another.

Such sideways energy creates a climate of tension instead of attention and frequent flares of annoyance instead of appreciation. It is aptly explained in Tim and Joy Downs' book *Fight Fair: Winning at Conflict Without Losing at Love*. What God labels as a partnership and a buffer against misunderstanding and miscommunication often disintegrates into selfishness and hopelessness.

Differences don't divide, but how we deal with differences does disconnect us. Every couple creates patterns of behavior to deal with the distance. Many stonewall because evasion feels better than being uncomfortable, but refusing to talk about a difficulty doesn't generate a door but a barrier. It's a ***stone wall***. Everything is not okay. Silence isn't a strategy. You must name your differences to tame the distance.

Fighting for one another
is better than fleeing or freezing.

NAME YOUR DIFFERENCES TO TAME THE DISTANCE

When I'm not at my best, rather than appreciating my wife for who she is, I become frustrated that she isn't me. Her differences annoy me because I'm convinced I'm a better creator than her Heavenly Father. Early in our marriage, I was trying to undo the way God gift-wrapped her personality to make her more like me.

Rather than receive her as a perfect gift from the giver of every good gift (James 1:17), I rejected His one-of-a-kind, custom-made provision for my life. I was, in essence, critiquing her Creator as uninspired and disorganized, and praying to her Heavenly Father to make my practical wife into a clone and a copy of me. I now shake my head at the audacity of such stupidity.

Instead, we need to look at ways to identify how God made us individually unique. We can name the differences to tame the distance. Think of ways God uses the differences in our mates to invigorate our lives and fortify our union. The purpose of discovering how our spouse differs from us is not to use the information to point out flaws, but to decrease the distance in our relationship.

Our lives can be made better by our differences, which:

- Force us to depend on God.
- Create complementary relationships.
- Foster intimacy.

Couples can find many ways to understand and accept their differences. I'm convinced many marriages put their best foot forward for about one year. Then, our authentic self emerges. It's usually somewhat surprising, much like cold feet under the sheets. Of course, some of us are overachievers and start much sooner.

Our first big melee occurred when putting icicles on a Christmas tree. These individual strands of long, silvery tinsel caught the reflections of the light on the tree. But they aren't sold anymore because they are hazardous to pets and crawling babies. Nancy was convinced each branch needed exactly three strands, which you grabbed exactly in the middle (tape measure optional). And that you then placed them exactly 1.29 inches from the tip (there may be a *slight* exaggeration in this retelling).

Sixteen hours later, the tree was perfect. Nancy also suggested carefully removing the metallic pieces and draping them back over the cardboard for the following year. It's partly why we have a fake tree with pre-lit lights (no needles or fire hazard, I'm told). I was convinced that grabbing a gob of icicles and using the "Random Clump Theory" was much more efficient.

You could quickly do a quarter of a package at a time. It took practice to perfect the grab and spread technique, but it would usually land in a maze of beauty. I *think* that's how it is—I only got to do it once (I joke).

The underlying differences that divided us in the first year included things like toothpaste tops, toilet lids, laundry hampers, dirty dishes, and how to handle hamsters. (I made the last one up!) We now know that our personalities and temperaments, mingled with our preferences, beliefs, fears, and values, increase the opportunity for disagreement. These differences spill over into every arena of life, including:

- Parenting styles
- Physical intimacy
- Finances
- Division of duties
- In-laws
- Leisure time
- Vacation
- How to spend free time

Mark and Jill Savage have included this and much more in their book *No More Perfect Marriages: Experience the Freedom of Being Real Together.* It's worth walking through with your spouse!

Nancy's underlying personality enjoys (even relishes) structure and order. She likes her ducks in a row and lots of lists. Nancy believes control in an uncertain world includes detailed instruction manuals instead of haphazardly putting together a playset. I have learned that improvising with a big bag of bolts, nuts, and screws is a comedy of errors.

Appreciating her wiring brings fascination instead of frustration and helps me learn how to live with an organizer—she wants to be in on the planning. She is not big on surprises, so she wants a heads-up that a surprise is in the works. On the other hand, I love bolts from the blue and believe variety is the spice of life.

How do you mesh "Go-with-the-flow-Joe" with "Work-the-plan-Nancy?" We've learned that one-flesh intimacy for us includes planned spontaneity to break relational gridlock. Since reading Tim and Joy Downs' book, *One of Us Must Be Crazy, and I'm Pretty Sure It's You: Making Sense of the Differences that Divide Us*, we've discovered a way to address our differences through "planned spontaneity."

Now, we make a plan that includes adding unstructured pieces to the agenda. Plans like going on road trips are generated and highlighted by AAA, with time built in for taking some side roads. Nancy has learned to chillax and distinguish areas where order is critical and where it is simply desirable, and I can still launch the icicles. I have learned that processing and planning pay huge dividends. Facts matter. Research helps. Spreadsheets are cool.

We are different people, showing how dissimilar we are. We have learned to live separate lives together, interwoven as one flesh. We live full lives apart, which energizes our life together. I run marathons. Nancy runs to Hobby Lobby. I go on crazy mission trips. She builds portable pantries. I thrive on social activities and parties. Nancy prefers Pinterest and privacy.

It's weird because Nancy is perceived as more friendly and outgoing, but such contact drains her. I recharge at football games, parties, church, or anywhere there's lots of interaction. She likes people and parties, but she's looking for an exit because they wear her to a nub. She measures how much energy it will require to hug everyone in the room, smile incessantly, and engage in small talk. Except for the hugging part, just writing this energizes me. I'm ready to go.

These differences in how we are energized also impact how we interact with one another. I need connection. Nancy needs space. I want the whole gang to come. She groans. I'll invite people to our house for an unplanned shindig after church, and she will lock the door (I'm kidding!).

It's really about her capacity to recharge. Her health challenges (psoriatic arthritis and fibromyalgia) compound the need. She doesn't have the stamina or the capacity to handle juggling multiple responsibilities or to say yes to tons of invitations.

This invitation for us to be the best version of ourselves means we respect each other enough to allow God to craft each of us into who He wants us to be.

Marriage isn't a *have-to* transaction
but a *get-to* interaction.

YOUR PERSONAL BLUEPRINTS

There are many tools to help you diagnose your differences and sketch out plans to navigate the rapids produced by the swirling currents of contrasting personalities. We find ourselves in white waters of conflict, gasping for air, navigating by feelings and unspoken rules that we call normal, but unable to catch our breath. Even here, differences will determine which paddle you pull out. Nancy prefers visual tools. I like verbal help. I prefer diagnostic tools with specific suggestions. Nancy likes discussions and reading out loud. PUH-LEASE.

The reality is, there are a bunch of blueprints to name the differences to tame the distance. Your personality influences every area of your life:

- The decisions you make
- How you solve problems
- The vocation you should choose
- The person you should marry
- The type of ministry God wants you to have to serve Him

Your personality even influences how you relate to God. Some people relate to God in a quiet, meditative, contemplative way. Others relate to God in a very emotional, loud way. We're just different!

Multitudes are familiar with love languages or currencies, which are unconscious assumptions about how love is expressed meaningfully. These investments of love fill our emotional bank accounts, which John and Julie Gottman refer to in *The Art and Science of Love*. These investments bring special delight because they express love in ways that fill our love tanks.

Tim Keller says we should make deposits that express love for our spouses because God did this for us. He references John 1:14:

> The Word became flesh
> and made his dwelling among us.
> We have seen his glory,
> the glory of the one and only Son,
> who came from the Father,
> full of grace and truth.
> JOHN 1:14 NIV

God demonstrated his love for us in human form in a way we could grasp. Tim's book, *The Meaning of Marriage: Facing the Complexities of Commitment with the Wisdom of God,* further compares meaningful deposits with God's love for us.

This is reciprocated in relationships when we express our love over the channels our mates are attuned to. Love is expressed in deliberate choices, and discernment is needed to provide love in the most appropriate way. Withholding love intentionally is particularly harmful, damaging what we should cherish.

My wife is refueled by acts of service (lovingly entitled chore play) and considers tent camping an act of service. I consider it akin to waterboarding, but it refuels her in ways I cannot explain. So, I put on my best camping gear and toast marshmallows in the wind. I use outdoor plumbing (no more squatty potties—don't ask) and wrap up in a swaddling cloth called a sleeping bag. On the other hand, I am fueled and fired up by gifts. DM me, and I will give you a list of suggestions.

Gary Chapman defines love languages in his book, *The Five Love Languages: The Secret to Love That Lasts.* Interactive profiles of the five love languages are available at www.5lovelanguages.com. He defines love languages as words of affirmation, quality time, acts of service, giving gifts, and physical touch for couples.

Love languages are open faucets of encouragement and affirmation that enable spouses to stay in love. According to Chapman, we fall in love with our partner for a reason. I still vividly recall, even after 45 years, falling in love with my wife in 1980. We were both coming out of our freshman year of college and had a solid friendship to build upon. I was immediately attracted to her beautiful brown eyes, gracious smile, and friendly personality. She was holy-moley guacamole with hot salsa to match. A whirlwind romance ensued, and we married a year later at the ripe old age of 19. We had something in common: we were both in love with *me!*

Falling in love leads to full buckets. Life, bills, and jobs soon ensue, and whether through neglect or inattention, the flow lessens to drips, and the levels in the love bucket dissipate. At the same time, irritating behaviors we overlooked initially create holes in the bottom of the bucket and drain away the accumulation of goodwill. Discover what fuels and fills your partner up while acknowledging what drains and strains your relationship. This is a concrete way of creating love handles for the long haul. Creating a list to display in a prominent place or using an app like Dr. Wyatt Fisher's "Keep the Glow" is a meaningful investment in your marriage. His book, *Total Marriage Refresh: 6 Steps to Marital Satisfaction,* provides more ideas for filling the bucket and how to stop the drain.

Another way to understand your differences is the study of "love styles." Individual imprints formed long ago to create a core pattern of how we either pursue one another or distance ourselves from the pursuit (www.howwelove.com). Milan and Kay Yerkovich explore these different styles in their book *How We Love: Discover Your Love Style, Enhance Your Marriage.* The love styles vary in the dance of love by either drawing close or pushing away in the dance of romance. And this often also means stepping on each other's toes. The goal is to discover a secure connection that uses healthy boundaries. And to ask for what we want rather than demanding that our partner live as we do.

I'm a vacillator, and Nancy is an avoider, which means Nancy needs space. I idealize the amount of connection that is possible. High expectations often disappoint us because they are impossible to meet. Diagnosing our differences began a quest to set internal and external boundaries. These boundaries allow us to become who God created us to be—not a replica or a copy, but authentic and genuine. In *Naked Marriage, Uncovering Who You Are and Who You*

Can Be Together, Corey Allen says we are partially to blame for how we are treated:

> If you tolerate your spouse's physical or emotional
> unavailability or their hurtful or abusive behavior,
> it's a fifty-fifty problem, even if you've never retaliated
> or made mention of the issue.
> Here's the kicker:
> You have no control over their fifty percent.
> But you do have a hundred percent control
> over your fifty percent.
> You alone oversee your emotions and reactions . . .
> you teach people how to treat you.
> Corey Allen

Boundaries help you lead yourself well, protect your marital relationship, and protect you from evil and foolishness.

This marital pursuit helps ease one of the perpetual problems of marriage: differences create distance. It likewise eases the steps taken by couples to repair the relationship. Differences force us to depend on God. Like the familiar song from the movie *Beauty and the Beast*:

> Tale as old as time . . . Both a little scared,
> Neither one prepared, Beauty and the Beast.
> Ariana Grande and John Legend

This pursuit and distance can create a situation where intimacy is negligible, and distance is substantial.

It began in a garden when God said something wasn't good. It's not good to be alone (Genesis 2:18). So, God crafted Eve from Adam's rib, and the chase was on. When Adam and Eve ate from the only tree off-limits in the middle of the garden, sin descended. It brought with it the possibility of disengagement, dismissal, and loneliness. Then, the eyes of the original couple were opened to their vulnerabilities, and they covered their hurt with fig leaves. *Quick Dad joke: Someone must wear the plants in the family!*

For the first time, they needed emotional safety, and defensiveness became a new reality. Rather than true intimacy, Adam and Eve hid from God and one another, and the blame game began. They didn't sing Taylor Swift's tune, "Antihero," with its lyrics: "It's me, hi, I'm the problem, it's me." Instead, they flipped the script and said, "It's not me. It's you."

Such defensiveness and blame led to a pattern that is constant in marriages. In his research, John Gottman found that most American husbands (65 percent) do not, in his words, "accept influence" from their wives. They disregard their wives' opinions, feelings, and concerns. They ignore, criticize, and drown out their wives' voices. They accuse them of overreacting (e.g., "You're too sensitive"). When men behave this way, not surprisingly, their wives feel disrespected and devalued.

Gottman states that this failure of a husband to share power with his partner means there is an 81% chance the marriage will end. Unfortunately, it will end either in divorce or perpetual unhappiness. (See Nancy Pearcey's book, *The Toxic War on Masculinity: How Christianity Reconciles the Sexes.*) That's disheartening, but such knowledge of a lack of respect for the wife's input is also a powerful lever that can change the course of the marriage. A lack of respect kills intimacy in marriage. Admiration decreases separation. There are tons of ways we can disrespect our partner. Our tone of voice, lack of attention, indifference to engaging, harsh words, and outright contempt can diminish hope. *Momentum can be built when small steps are taken to rebuild lost respect.*

Partners must open the lines of communication and drop the crowbars of manipulation and intimidation. Manipulation tactics are sneaky tendencies that hide in the darkness and emerge at the most inopportune times.

Selena Frederick, in her book *How a Wife Speaks: Loving Your Husband Well through Godly Communication,* states that we can treat the other spouse like a child through patronizing, sarcastic, or condescending language. We can stonewall our spouse with the silent treatment to cut off conversation and punish our spouse. We can invalidate our spouse by casually dismissing the source of contention. Manipulation may also include evidence from friends that makes our spouse feel like they are on the wrong side of the issue. Manipulation kills momentum.

Creating momentum requires that someone takes the initiative to close the intimacy gap. Empirical research and biblical wisdom coalesce to offer a way to bridge the divide. Particularly when the husband takes the initiative to repair the relationship (more on this in the next chapter). In her book, S. Frederick recalls this quote by Tim Challies:

A husband's leadership is not first a matter of breaking ties or solving impasses but a matter of being the first to love, the first to serve, the first to repent, the first to forgive.
Tim Challies

Human marriage emulates the pattern of Jesus and his bride: "We love because he first loved us" (1 John 4:19 [NIV]).

Most women want closeness, while men crave control. David Clarke refers to these two roles in his book, *Men Are Clams, Women Are Crowbars: Understand Your Differences and Make Them Work.* Some couples flip-flop these roles; the woman is the clam, and the man is the crowbar. But regardless, the principle is still the same: intimacy is the activity that closes the distance. The key is discovering the unprocessed emotions that cause distance. Intimacy occurs when you process those emotions and create a connection. Differences that created distance are now drafted to become emotional connectors.

One of my favorite profiles is in Mark and Jill Savage's book *No More Perfect Marriages: Experience the Freedom of Being Real Together*. It classifies personality disparities as operating systems that run in the background. They can create gaps and discord if not acknowledged. Unaddressed dissimilarities create dissonance and dissatisfaction that often settle into bitterness and are expressed in rejection, which puts miles between our hearts. This little quiz, available at www.nomoreperfectmarriages.com, helps each spouse create a gauge for how they process the world around them.

It is telling that Nancy and I are opposites in each dynamic but one. We are both feelers instead of thinkers. She's an external processor who gives a play-by-play description of most events she encounters. She talks through what she wants to do. Sometimes, it can be a word salad I cannot eat.

I'm an internal processor. I can think about something for days and then tell Nancy what we are doing. I tend to allow my thoughts to marinate with no commentary. I assume Nancy knows what I'm thinking, but you know what they say about assuming.

Other dynamics have already been detailed: She's structured, and I'm spontaneous. She organizes our pantry by the alphabet, and I am chasing squirrels. I'm wired with a high capacity to juggle a lot emotionally and need little recovery time before the next project. I unpack my bags the minute I walk in the door and am ready immediately for the next trip. Nancy needs one project or a trip at a time until she is finished. Then she needs sleep and a spa.

Several other profiles are less DIY and are done with trained coaches. Les and Leslie Parrott use the SYMBIS (Saving Your Marriage Before It Starts) assessment. It's phenomenal and based on empirical research (www.symbis.com). A self-assessment is available at www.betterlove.com. Prepare and Enrich is another vehicle that uses trained facilitators and is accessible at https://www.prepare-enrich.com.

FEARFULLY AND WONDERFULLY MADE

Paul David Tripp gives stellar advice in *Marriage: 6 Gospel Commitments Every Couple Needs to Make*. He says that each spouse should celebrate their Creator instead of denigrating their spouse. Refuse to see differences as right or wrong. This is what the Creator hard-wired into our spouses.

> When we begin to think our hard-wiring makes us better,
> more mature, or more righteous than our spouse,
> we will act and respond in ways
> that are dismissive and disrespectful.
> Paul David Tripp

Instead, we can use admiration and appreciation for how meticulous and scrupulous God is in crafting our spouse. Irritation and frustration in the face of differences reveal our thinly disguised attempts to manipulate a mindset. Hoping our husbands get the hint doesn't bring harmony. Wishing our wives would see it our way doesn't create intimacy. These attitudes really say we don't receive our mates as the instrument God intends to use to sharpen and hone us to be more like Jesus.

Constant critiques of differences create hostility instead of intimacy. God designed marriage to be the place of our greatest blessing rather than the space of our deepest hurts. Everybody needs a cheerleader. Everybody needs to hear the words, "Good job." Deep down, we desire affirmation and "attaboys."

Nobody likes constant boos, according to Dave and Ann Wilson in *Vertical Marriage: The One Secret that Will Change Your Marriage.* Our mates cherish our cheers and are motivated by our applause. It's not an excuse to avoid hard conversations and speak the truth in love. Still, it is an exercise in prudence and diligence to create an atmosphere in our homes that makes them a place we desire to be.

Think of ways to praise the way God made your mate rather than criticize them for differing from you. Instead of trying to convince them that your ways are best, allow them to be who God designed them to be. This cannot be fake flattery or manufactured manipulation, but genuine praise that conveys appreciation and brings validation.

My dad rarely showed me this growing up. Thus, winning the state basketball championship in high school remains a vivid and cherished memory. I distinctly remember my dad pushing security guards aside, coming to the gym floor of the Super Drum in Austin, and saying two short sentences. "I love you. I am proud of you." Even as I write these words, my heart swells.

Nancy Pearcey notes in her book, *The Toxic War on Masculinity,* that too many men missed this affirmation and resent that they cannot receive from their wives what they need from their dads. And Gordon Dalbey says this in *Healing the Masculine Soul: How God Restores Men to Real Manhood*:

> Men today desperately need the saving grace
> and truth of the God who manifests as Father,
> in order not only to become secure in our manhood,
> [cont'd next page]

TOUGH TALKS

> but to come alongside
> and bless women as true partners
> in our common destiny.
> Gordon Dalbey

Our Heavenly Father affirmed Jesus with these words:

> This is my Son, whom I love;
> with him I am well pleased.
> MATTHEW 3:17B NIV

These were the last words Jesus heard from His Father before His 40 days of wilderness temptation. I'm convinced the applause of heaven prepared Him for the attack in the desert. Don't doubt the fact that your words of hope can create all kinds of momentum. Overdo the compliments. Look for the best in your partner. Words have enormous weight and are not just a tagline. Words create a lifeline.

Lifelines allow us to shift into the next phase of marriage: relational health. Relational health is found in spiritual maturity and emotional stability. These "shifts" require engaging your spouse with empathy and active listening. Every marriage can find lanes to travel in where relational wrecks are avoided, adversarial logjams are dodged, and marital intimacy accelerates. It starts with a shift.

Chapter 3

Start-Ups and Clutches

Relationships progress as you learn to engage the clutch of your faith, shift attentive listening into gear, accelerate conversations with empathy, and repeat the shifts. My book, *Love Handles*, discusses minor "shifts" needed for maintaining connections with your spouse. Couples don't create marriages through grand gestures, but they do so by shifting their attention towards each other daily in the small stuff. To quote from my teaching:

> Healthy couples downshift the gears of their minds to an awareness of the need to engage with their spouse with interest, rather than dead silence, dismissive indifference, or passive ill will...
> We need to shift out of Park and move into connection.
> Dr. Joe Stewart, *Love Handles*

Let's explore the four essential gears that drive a marriage and facilitate closeness.

FIRST GEAR: THE SOFT START-UP

First gear is the art of "the soft start-up" when making or responding to a bid for connection. This concept comes from John Gottman's book, *The Art and Science of Love*. A soft start-up means we treat our spouse with the same respect and courtesy as we treat houseguests when initiating communication. Soft startups recognize that how something begins determines what will ensue during the discussion. The soft start-up helps decompress stress as we ease into the conversational gear.

Stress from work, friends, kids, and external factors can substantially drain love buckets, and your husband or wife can be a place for deposits made that refill the bucket. Consistent deposits can accumulate for when life gets difficult later.

Proverbs 15:1 (NLT) says, "A gentle answer deflects anger, but harsh words make tempers flare." A relationship expert, John Gottman, identifies a love handle in the first three minutes of conversation. In *The Art and Science of Love*, he describes how he differentiates between those who are masters of relationships and those who are disasters. According to research, the first three minutes of a discussion predict the outcome of the entire dialogue. When we practice gentle beginnings, we turn towards one another instead of turning away.

Many times, conversations begin with complaints. Complaints can quickly become personal, and we can use an arsenal of stored memories to become historical (and hysterical). Nancy and I don't have nearly as many knock-down drag outs as we did early on in our marriage, as we mend quarrels much more quickly. However, we still know how to put on our fighting gloves and get in the ring. We forget the rules of interpersonal conflict and try to use our words to score a knockdown and win a fight. These marital matches often break out when we fail to ask God to serve as our coach and advocate.

H.A.L.T

We had a doozy of an argument the night before a marriage seminar in Spain. It's ironic that I was moronic on the night before we had to speak together on marriage. Round one started on the flight out of the United States, as scheduling snafus made our departure a bit snippy.

I leaned over at the gate and whispered in her ear, "I'm not sure what's wrong, but you've been a grouch and a grinch these past few days." That's when the gloves came off, and she tersely replied, "You are out of your ever-loving skull." (It's how I remember it anyhow.) "What planet are you living on?"

My courteous and well-mannered reply came next. "You've seemed irritated. I feel like I can't do anything to please you." Then, she does what I hate and asks for specific examples when I barely remember what I had for breakfast. I can never access details promptly, which leads to the conclusion that I've got nothing.

The next few rounds occurred with terse verbal sparring as we made quick connections to Barcelona. We didn't avail ourselves of any spiritual managers in our corner, so we failed to get instructions between the bells. We know how we are supposed to argue, but when unplanned melees break out, we often resort to brawling.

We have a better understanding because we teach that most fights start when we should "H.A.L.T." to see if we are:

- **Hungry**
- **Angry**

- **L**onely
- **T**ired

We landed in Spain, fulfilling all four criteria, and the bell rang for the final round. Nancy wanted to head straight to the terminal for our final leg. I wanted a burrito.

I took off in the conversation with no consideration for gentle starts, letting Nancy know in no uncertain terms that she was acting like the northbound end of a southbound donkey. *That's pastoral lingo.* The African killer bees came out of the hive of her heart. We crashed on the conversational runway without any landing gear. It was interesting to teach sixty Spanish couples about starting with a tender tone the next day. FAIL.

Rather than loving one another, we were taking bare-knuckle swings at one another. Such a stance attacks rather than attracts. It repels rather than compels. Nancy turned the tide with this doozy. "Why are we fighting each other when we should be fighting for one another? The enemy (Satan) is in the other corner, trying to disqualify both of us."

She showed me some better moves in the ring, led by the rhythms of grace.

We gradually lowered our gloves, looked each other in the eyes, and remembered that we were partners instead of rivals. Her decision to stop swinging allowed me to gather my composure and compliment Nancy for how she attempts to match my pace during marriage retreats. I vocalized that I appreciate it when she accompanies me for the highlight and headline events because she sparkles and shimmers. She polishes up nicely. She responded with a hug, kiss, and three soft words, "I love you." Conflict defused.

B.E.S.T.

Gentle beginnings are a learned skill akin to shifting into first gear, and it isn't automatic to turn criticisms into complaints. We all have grievances, but how we communicate our gripes needs careful thought. Constant criticism is nitpicking. Fussy, fault-finding, and quibbling erode trust, chip away at confidence, diminish intimacy, and belittle the other person. It's worth repeating that Proverbs 15:1 suggests, "A gentle answer turns away wrath, but a harsh word stirs up anger." Stinging criticism escalates conflict and damages relationships, whereas a tender answer is a soothing balm.

The odds of patching up a relational tear are greater when the startup is softer. This doesn't mean every conflict is resolved. In fact, most relational conflicts aren't solvable, according to John Gottman in his book *The Art and Science of Love.* Many of the marital issues couples face are perpetual, recurring over and over and over again. These issues are rooted in the way we handle life on subjects like punctuality, sexual intimacy, or handling money. We have profound differences that make us incompatible. *Everyone* is incompatible.

Tim and Joy Downs state in *Fight Fair*, "Compatibility is not a lack of differences; it's your attitude towards the differences." Learning to navigate these marital speed bumps will lead to mutual understanding. This leads to loving each other better, renewing our commitment with deeper resolve, and emotionally attaching at deeper levels. It's not a given that you can ease into actions that facilitate bids for connection. Good intentions don't always translate into intended outcomes.

One of our favorite cities is Vancouver, in British Columbia. The thriving city is situated on a beautiful harbor with a moderate climate and spectacular views. Stanley Park is at the end of the peninsula on the edge of downtown and is a 1000-acre tranquil oasis in the urban landscape. This Canadian haven is encircled by a seawall that offers magnificent views of the North Shore mountains and the Lions Gate Bridge. The six-mile circle is a paved path framed by giant trees, rose gardens, and scenic beaches that bikers and hikers can navigate. We decided to explore this green wonderland during our first foray on electric bikes.

We rented the bikes, got fitted with helmets, got a quick rundown on how to engage the different levels of assistance in pedaling, and began our tour. Each assist level offers a boost in power that engages the bike's motor. This allows our physical pedaling to diminish and the bike's motor to kick in with an additional increase in assistance.

Halfway through our loop, I nonchalantly asked Nancy what level she was using. I learned she did three miles with the assistance level at zero. I was amazed she could keep pace with my athletic physique, but she barely broke a sweat. She shifted her assistance level to High and subsequently left me in the dust. She was making do, but she found her best gear halfway in.

We find our best gear for connection when we invite God into every shift in our marital journey. Praying is the warm-up activity that fuels understanding, increases intimacy, and lubricates the conversations that remove friction in marital relationships. The start-up is smoother when God is in the gears. Rather than relying on our actions and being guided solely by intuition, we shift to the grace, wisdom, and insight offered by our Heavenly Father. Only then can we be at our B.E.S.T.

- **B**ody Language
- **E**nthusiasm
- **S**ense of Humor
- **T**one

There are dozens of everyday moments where what we say does not matter nearly as much as how we convey what we say. Nonverbal cues and clues speak loudly and clearly without saying a word. Every moment and movement matters. Every interaction counts.

Facial expressions don't lie. Leaning in declares a decision. Open hands invite us in. Eyes can look away, look off, look down, or look in. We need to look *in,* to lock *on.* Pursed lips say nope. Crossed arms and legs echo a similar response. A slouched posture speaks volumes about our level of engagement. Don't sigh or roll your eyes because every action either gains traction and fills our partner's love tank or subtracts from the emotional reservoir of our hearts.

Enthusiastic responses to our partner's attempts at engagement don't have to mean we whoop or cheer when a bid is made. Still, we need to respond actively and enthusiastically. I've learned that it's ok to yell, "WHOO-HOO!" when Nancy shares good news, just as I do when my favorite team wins a game. Nancy is good at celebrating and commiserating. I'm low-key and must intentionally amplify my response several levels to match Nancy's intensity. Positive responses of interest and support provide pedal assists in the longevity and strength of our marriages.

I know it's out of sequence in the acronym, but tone of voice is a valuable predictor of marital success. How we say something really, really matters. Ask any teenager. Using a warm, positive, and enthusiastic tone when speaking is an immediate love handle we can employ that greatly enhances our percentage of marital happiness. Positive voice tones defuse tense conflict, increase marital harmony, demonstrate emotional intelligence, and build stronger relationships. Many women are especially put off by harsh tones and hateful inflections that use the tongue as a concealed weapon, doing tremendous damage. Asking your mate and your Creator to help you turn up or turn down your tone appropriately is an excellent step toward intimacy.

Another practice that helps energize marital harmony is maintaining a sense of humor. Many people discourage marital teasing, but we always use playful banter. The secret humor between us usually involves my using the art of the double entendre. This makes me chuckle, but gains barely a hint of a smile from Nancy (usually a reserved "hmmm").

My wisecracks are a lot like the asparagus left too long in the fridge: a little limp and hard to digest. There's an art to the one-liner: it needs to be delivered at the perfect time with a subtle slide into the conversation. We love to laugh, and we use humor to defuse tense situations. The truth is, our marriage is a lot of things, but boring isn't our buzzword.

How do we survive and thrive? We recast each other's irritating behaviors into amusing anecdotes. She'll call my tendency to pout pitiful, and we'll both giggle. I'll talk about her organizational skills, such as alphabetizing the pantry, and she'll smirk. It's not hurtful. It's a way to see each other's differences in a new light. Rather than becoming frustrated or irritated, we accept each other, warts and all. Rather than wishing our spouse would change, we are committed to loving each other where we are and as we are.

So, let's refuse to cast our spouse in a negative light and instead appreciate each other as irreplaceable. Decide to stress the positive and depreciate the negative and communicate that we are each other's one and only. Intervene with a decision to believe the best about each other, with the bottom-line belief that we would choose each other all over again.

Proverbs 18:21 (NIV) says, "The tongue has the power of life and death, and those who love it will eat its fruit." Constructive words build up. Destructive words tear down. Positive phrases breathe life. Negative bruises create hurt. Hurtful words show hate. Healing words bring hope. Try it. Look at your mate. Breathe life. Exhale hope. Shift into a positive gear.

SECOND GEAR: LISTEN ATTENTIVELY AND RESPOND APPROPRIATELY

Second gear is the groove of a fluid connection. Manual transmissions do their job through plenty of metal-to-metal contacts, so they need a load of lubricant to soften touch points and keep everything running smoothly. This communication gear engages our ears more than our mouths and listens with our heart and head. The lubricant of love keeps the gears from grinding and verbal transmissions from slipping. Using the clutch is like pausing for a nanosecond to allow God to filter our thoughts and respond gracefully.

Effective connection is like a game of catch. Bids for connection require reading all the cues and clues demonstrated in various fashions. Second gear is learning to listen attentively and respond appropriately. The bid might begin with a verbal toss that is light and easy to catch rather than bearing down with a fiery spoken fastball. Every spouse needs to learn to listen, catch the gist of what was said, and pitch back an appropriate response. Some couples even practice with beanbags. Soft tosses only! Proverbs 15:23 says,

> A person finds joy in giving an apt reply—
> and how good is a timely word!
> PROVERBS 15:23 NIV

The New Living Translation also connects:

> Everyone enjoys a fitting reply; it is wonderful to say
> the right thing at the right time!
> PROVERBS 15:23 NLT

A fitting reply starts with listening. Listening is love. Proverbs. 12:15 is instructive:

> The way of fools seems right to them,
> but the wise listen to advice.
> PROVERBS 12:15 NIV

Accepting bids and deep listening bring back a piece of Paradise in a broken world. The healing bids reverse the curse rather than fracture the soul.

Nancy is a master of the fitting reply. She connects with her daughters, grandsons, friends, and husband (that's me) with artful grace. Her superpower is deep concentration. She doesn't let distractions keep her from being fiercely present in the moment. She concentrates. She communicates. She doesn't abbreviate her time or her attention. She's attuned. It's incredible to watch as she kneels to get a toddler's attention and sits down to talk to a grieving widow. Nancy lets you know she's heard you, feels you, and gets you. She knows how to shift into a lower and slower gear to stay connected in the moment.

This ability is a learned skill. It's the art of engaging the clutch. The clutch disconnects the engine's power from your wheels so you can change gears and use the accelerator. Use too little gas and the engine will stall. Using the clutch, especially on hills, requires intense focus. It's a bit tricky to get the hang of using the clutch, engaging the brake, making the shift, and using the accelerator. Driving a manual transmission takes a ton of practice.

Listening also requires effort, intentionality, and a lot of repetition. I often get distracted by deciding what to say in response to a conversation while juggling several tasks simultaneously. The key is listening to understand and contemplate rather than listening to invalidate and dominate. Using verbal brakes engages the gift of soothing silence. Proverbs 10:19 says,

> Too much talk leads to sin.
> Be sensible and keep your mouth shut.
> PROVERBS 10:19 NLT

This isn't an excuse to disengage, but it's a reminder to slow down and think carefully before you speak (according to Tim and Joy Downs in *Fight Fair: Winning in Conflict Without Losing in Love)*. When the pace of a passionate discussion accelerates, engage the clutch, hit the brakes, and shift to a lower gear. Take a breath, give it a rest, and make sure the words you use are the words you choose.

Silence lets you pause. Silence should signal to your partner that interruption isn't helpful. Silence permits you to park and ponder. Silence pursues peace. It prevents rash, harsh, and empty words. Calming your mind allows you to speak soothing, gracious, timely, and pleasant words.

All this talk about driving reminds me of a perpetual problem you've already heard about that exists in our marriage. *I love you, Honey, but I can't stand your driving.* Nancy once pointed out a bumper sticker that said, "Yeah, my driving scares me, too."

My driving often makes her feel unsafe. I think it's because I totaled a Land Cruiser in a parking lot. Nancy gets in the passenger seat, quickly cinches her seatbelt, grabs the side handle, and ensures her airbag works. She also checks to see if her oxygen mask will drop and if her barf bag is readily available. She suggests I make her car sick.

My problem is that I see yellow lines as suggestions, road signs as obnoxious, and driving as secondary to other endeavors. Yet, we had just finished a road trip with zero conflict over this subject, and

Nancy was riding shotgun. How? We've learned the art of the second shift. It goes something like this:

- *I feel.* She says, "I feel unsafe when you grab your phone while driving." The words, *I feel,* begin a simple statement that carries incredible benefits, as it keeps the focus on feelings and your perspective rather than judging or accusing.
- *I need.* She gently explains her needs, as I cannot read her mind. "I need you to slow down."
- *I appreciate.* She verbalizes appreciation that defuses tension. "I appreciate your keeping both hands on the wheel." Appreciation builds affection. So does letting Nancy drive.

Proverbs 18:13 (NLT) frames a path forward:

> Spouting off before listening to the facts is both shameful and foolish.
> PROVERBS 18:14 NLT

Man, have I been a blowhole way too often, a verbal geyser spewing who knows what when I needed to clamp it down. I can think of instances where my first response is, "Yeah, I know." It's worse when I say, "Well, that's obvious." That quickly helps some gears to shift, and not in a positive way.

In *How a Wife Speaks,* Selena Frederick explains that marital unity requires that couples realize they no longer have the freedom to say whatever they want, however or whenever they want. We need to quit being blowholes and start progressing towards becoming a Pro Bowl communicator.

Second gear is not listening to reload. Second gear listens to learn. Proverbs 18:15 advises:

DR. JOE STEWART

> Intelligent people are always ready to learn.
> Their ears are open for knowledge.
> **PROVERBS 18:15 NLT**

You listen instead of interrupting. Close the gap. Hit the brakes. Watch God keep us from spinning our wheels. Then, shift into the next gear to accept a bid for connection. *We will soon find ourselves on an adventure we never saw coming.*

Chapter 4

Hellos and Goodbyes

There's an iconic movie moment in the movie *Jerry Maguire* that generates the classic line, "You had me at 'Hello,'" which has been skewered by pastors and marriage experts as way off base. Yet, it is true that spouses can have their partner at hello. We generate tons of traction in our marriage with the way we say hello and goodbye.

THIRD GEAR: SHIFTING INTO EMOTIONAL SUPPORT

Third gear is the momentum of moments that increase understanding. Couples need to be aware of unintentionally veering out of the lane of emotional support. This requires traveling in two lanes: owning our brokenness and learning to name, recognize, and acknowledge our feelings. (NOTE: There are some non-negotiables where a partner needs to get away from the environment because of abuse, violence, addiction, or volatility.)

Tim and Joy Downs, in *Fight Fair,* explain the following. Too often, the exceptionally verbal spouse will live by the motto, "If you want to know what I mean, listen to what I say." The other spouse feels that level of directness is too blunt, so their dictum speaks, "If you want to know what I mean, watch for how I feel." We often talk past one another rather than connect with one another.

These misfired connections can create a volatile environment where a single spark can set things off. The reality is that some couples interact defensively because they are on edge and aren't giving their partners the benefit of the doubt. Many spouses shut down because previous attempts to connect are rebuffed, and pretending seems better than vulnerability that might lead to dissension. The assumption is that it is better to sweep difficulties under the rug than to deal with issues. Some spouses tidy this up by labeling this "keeping peace" and turning to the beatitudes as a bumper sticker where Jesus says, "Blessed are the peacemakers" (Matthew 5:9a [NIV]).

Keeping peace and making peace are entirely different, as peacemaking glues couples together, and peacekeeping eventually pushes spouses apart. Keeping peace is a strategy of avoidance that minimizes conflict and diminishes the importance of the avoider's feelings. Such a stance usually causes resentment and erodes the relationship. Shifting into a position of emotional support is an undertaking that will build collaboration and create a positive culture of validation.

These love handles for making peace are practical, but it doesn't mean they are easy to employ. A blissful afternoon floating a lazy river on the same inner tube can instantly turn to navigating conversational rapids with no escape route. I still remember the summer day we plopped into the vinyl seat. It was blissful until my harmless response about her friend having a point created lots of relational waves.

The whitecaps crested when a stirred-up wife suggested I wasn't on her side. We went to our corners and came out swinging. Internally, I contemplated throwing her off the tube without a life jacket. Maybe she would forget how to swim while alligators stirred the stream, as I threw chum in the water and prayed snapping turtles would join the frenzy. This doesn't build rapport. I learned that unfiltered remarks should not be shared, and some settings and times are better than others. An inner tube, on a hot summer day, on a lazy river, does not qualify as the time or the place. Such a reminder keeps alligators out of our thoughts.

Proverbs 18:2 (NIV) says, "Fools find no pleasure in understanding but delight in airing their own opinions." Nancy needed someone on her side. I threw her emotions overboard because I wasn't focused on trying to understand. I was reloading my own judgments and airing them fully. I'm lucky she didn't have an oar, a taser, a chainsaw, or snapping turtles. We stayed in the tube because we had promised on our wedding day and every anniversary since not to bail, so we decided to hear each other out.

Listening to understand rather than to be understood. It's much like communicating through walkie-talkies. We push the button, and when we are done, we say, "Over." The response comes as we process the message, with the feedback coming, "Over." Understanding does not come in interaction until the message sent is the message received. Over.

DRIVE-THROUGH FEEDBACK

We often must communicate using the McDonald's drive-through process and repeat what's been said until the message gets through.

I sometimes speak softly in the drive-through and then must raise my voice level until I feel they can hear me in Montreal. I'll repeat my order until I get my Big Mac, hold the bun. I don't understand why the knuckleheads on the other side of the fast-food speaker cannot understand the concise, crystal-clear orders I articulate as the verbal wordsmith I am.

Once, in Nogales, Arizona, when I was trying to order at KFC, they could not grasp a single word I used to get my point across. Their chosen language was Spanish. Mine seemed to be gibberish. They had me drive to the window, and every employee at the establishment looked out to see what the redneck was blubbering over the speaker. IT WAS HILARIOUS. I finally got my chicken.

It's not so comical when we do this in our marriage. We craft what we consider a master statement of connection, and then we conclude our spouse is too thick-headed to know what we are talking about. There is always a language gap that must be bridged. When miscommunication happens, the correct path is to keep repeating what we already said until it's heard. We recapitulate and reiterate until it resonates. Then we do it again in case they haven't figured it out. Colossians 4:6 says:

> Be gracious in your speech. The goal is
> to bring out the best in others in a conversation,
> not put them down, not cut them out.
> COLOSSIANS 4:6 (MSG)

Our mates will cut out if we cut them out. Our spouses will feel let down if we put them down.

Emotional connection is increased by seeking collaboration before problem-solving or giving advice. It's like when your child skinned their knee. Comfort first. Console at the beginning. Connect when they fall. Solutions to prevent a future fall can come later. Our husbands and wives need us to be emotional allies as we convey that we get it and get them. Even if the emotions seem out of whack or a little out there, it's still how they feel, and it's real. Supportive communication cements our emotional bond when a bid for connection is made.

We should never withhold appreciation because gratefulness fuels motivation for a better tomorrow. I love a line in the 1997 movie *As Good as It Gets*. An obsessive-compulsive romance novel author, Melvin Udall (played by Jack Nicholson), is enamored with a struggling waitress, Carol Connelly (played by Helen Hunt). She sees Melvin at his worst, yet agrees to meet him at a Michelin-rated restaurant for a date.

He is crass and insensitive, and Carol looks him in the eyes and says, "Pay me a compliment, Melvin. I need one now."

He delivers one of the most romantic lines in big-screen history as a flawed and awkward human. "Carol, you make me want to be a better man."

She replies, "That's maybe the best compliment of my life."

They are mismatched, like every couple on the planet, but they make each other aspire to improve. Do we want to make our mates better? Do we desire to share our hurts and hang-ups to lead to a better tomorrow? An emotional connection will invigorate relational health.

LOVING YOUR MATE WELL

Emotional support uses key love handles to facilitate intimacy. Part of the game is emotional intelligence. I Peter 3:7 frames it like this:

> In the same way, you husbands
> must give honor to your wives. [cont'd next page]

> Treat your wife with understanding as you live
> together. She may be weaker than you are,
> but she is your equal partner in God's gift of new life.
> Treat her as you should so your prayers
> will not be hindered.
> 1 PETER 3:9 NLT

That's a lot to unpack!

- Give honor to your wives.
- Treat your wife with understanding as you live together.
- She is an equal partner in God's gift of new life.
- Treat her with understanding so that your prayers won't be hindered.

Some assumptions permeate this passage. Spouses live together. It's not a junior high lock-in that you endure because you know the smells and the yells leave at 6 am. Your partner is permanent, like leftover chicken spaghetti. If that's too harsh, substitute filet mignon. The point is, our mates stay. It's not a sleepover or Netflix and chill. It's forever.

How we treat our spouse impacts the entire house. Honor is a noun that is lived as a verb. It's the cherishing part of our vows. Honor is meant to be GIVEN, not assumed. Honor is a gift. Our spouses are gifts. Happiness is a gift. Life is a gift. Honor should be given in every circumstance by a husband to his wife. It's in the vows:

> For better or worse, for richer or poorer,
> in sickness and in health, to love and to cherish,
> 'til death do you part.

Your "I do" means honor is due. This goes a long way in carrying your relationship past early giggly feelings of romantic love through alligator-infested waters. Your wife is an equal partner in God's gift (there's that word again) of new life.

Partners have a full say and vested interest. Equal partners cooperate and collaborate to bring profit to the enterprise. Too many spouses (often husbands) desire silent or limited partners who make significant investments in the marriage but get little say in the day-to-day decisions. Your wife is an equal, not a sequel, which is never as good as the original.

I must undertake a lifelong investigation of my wife to understand how she is wired. Thus, I can love her well where she lives and employ the full force of the power of prayer. Sometimes, I'm a dunderhead, but I want to tap into God as a fully invested partner in our marriage. Treating my mate as an equal partner invites God into our marriage with unlimited power and provision. I can quickly pivot from treating Nancy with decency and empathy as an equal partner and person to viewing her as a nuisance and noise.

Once, when attending a football game, I urged (advised, insisted, convinced, persuaded) Nancy to leave her blanket in the car. She left her pleasant mood in there as well. I was afraid the blanket would become my burial shroud. My attempt to control Nancy backfired, rapidly diminishing my influence and harming our relationship.

Emotional intelligence teaches that our partners' positions are valid and valued. Constantly demeaning or diminishing our mate's stance doesn't enhance emotional health. Instead, disrespect shrinks the quality of interaction and connection. I tend to undervalue Nancy's emotions because I suppress mine as invalid and intrusive, rather than a sign of something going on in my soul.

My solution at the football game was an attempt to persuade her that the disagreement was all her fault and that she was overreacting—wrong move. I fumbled my initial stab at persuasion. I wasn't loving her well.

Emotional health is deeply intertwined with spiritual flourishing. Consider Peter Scazzero's insight in his book, *Emotionally Healthy Spirituality: It's Impossible to be Spiritually Mature While Remaining Emotionally Immature.* Acknowledging what is happening inside us is indispensable in dealing with those around us.

Early in our marriage, my refusal to deal with emotions caused a distance between my wife and me. I saw feelings as interruptions to life rather than the issue at hand. I thought I was loving Nancy well, but the problem was that my feelings were the issue, and ignoring them was nearly impossible. Often, discussions about sexual frequency were more about feelings of rejection and hurt surfacing from deep layers in my soul.

Rather than acknowledge my feelings to Nancy (which I saw as a weakness), I would pop off phrases in anger. It's like dropping a can of Dr. Pepper and immediately popping the top. It can be messy. Counseling enabled me to see my emotions as invitations to intimacy with my wife and not barriers to marital health.

Jesus demonstrated His authentic self: "He began to be sorrowful and troubled. Then he said to them, 'My soul is overwhelmed with sorrow, to the point of death,'" (Matthew 26:37b-38a [NIV]). Jesus also expressed anger, joy, love, and a gamut of emotions. Spouses' emotions are often suppressed rather than expressed, and mates are unaware rather than self-aware. We are constantly clueless about emotional health, rather than cued in about how a healthy *me* leads to a healthy *us*. Many people only know two emotions: mad and sad— especially mad—which can be toxic in a marriage.

LOOK UNDER THE HOOD

I'm not super mechanical, but I've learned that when the radiator is hissing and the coolant warning light is illuminated, it's an almost sure sign the engine is overheating. In a minuscule number of cases, the sensor might malfunction. However, you still must do a diagnostic test to discover the glitch.

Ignoring the gauge and continuing to drive is a definite no. Ask me how I know. You must pull to the side of the road, stop the car, pop the hood, and wait a while before relieving the pressure on the radiator cap. Refusal to do so can lead to permanent engine damage and expensive repairs. Billowing white smoke escaping from the exhaust isn't a sign of the election of a new pope; however, it's often a symbol of a blown head gasket. Another little aside: wait a while before you open the radiator cap. It will prevent some severe pain.

Anger is a similar sign on the dashboard of your soul, indicating something is wrong that needs to be made right. Tim and Joy Downs address anger in their book *Fight Fair*. The wrong approach is continuing a conversation while emotionally overheated, as you say a lot without saying anything. Too often in marital conversations, we blow a gasket in sudden anger, release some steam, and do enormous damage to the one we love the most. Repairing the relationship then costs more and works less.

On the road to greater intimacy, the Bible says,

> People with understanding control their anger;
> a hot temper shows great foolishness.
> PROVERBS 14:29 NLT

We always lose when we lose our temper. Much can be forfeited, including our jobs, relationships, and reputation. We need to pull over to the side of the road metaphorically. "Wise people think before they act; fools don't," (Proverbs 13:16 [NLT]). We then pop the hood to our hearts and depend on God to search us and heal our hurts. We need Him to replace our frustration and insecurity with God-given identity.

Remember that pulling over means a time-out (at least thirty minutes) before you reengage. Trying to resolve a situation when the radiator of your heart is overheating will only cause serious pain. This routine takes into consideration the biblical guidelines on anger: "In your anger do not sin. Do not let the sun go down while you are still angry, and do not give the devil a foothold" (Ephesians 5:26-27).

Nancy and I used to stay up until the wee hours of the morning in a sincere attempt to honor God's counsel. In the end, we violated every segment of this Scripture. We would sin in our anger. The sun was already down and, in some cases, about to come up again, and the devil was in our bedroom. We learned to postpone the conversation and re-engage with better clarity and a less heated frame of mind.

The solution to anger isn't learning to vent—that too often scalds and blisters those closest to you. Proverbs 15:18 frames it in this fashion: "A hot-tempered person stirs up conflict, but the one who is patient calms a quarrel." *Difficult Conversations: How to Discuss What Matters Most,* by Douglas Stone, Bruce Patton, and Sheila Heen, outlines ways to express emotions thoughtfully.

It's interesting how emotions and self-control are intertwined to make an effective discussion more likely. Thinking about how you feel and feeling through how you think creates a path forward. Feelings follow thoughts. Emotions greatly color thoughts. Negotiating with your emotions before a commotion is better than spouting off or blowing your top.

> Our anger may lose its edge; our hurt may run less deeply;
> our feelings of betrayal or abandonment or shame
> or anxiety may feel more manageable.
> Feelings often change over time.
> We can be an active participant in shifting our stories,
> and adjusting our emotional reactions to those stories.
> Stone, Patton, Heer

- *Admit Your Fits.* Even when you think anger seems misplaced, admit your fits. The emotions may make us uncomfortable and seem irrational, but they still exist.
- *Get Angry with Clarity.* Examine the full spectrum of your emotional bandwidth. Spin the wheel to see how you feel. (Wheels of emotions are absolutely available.)
- *Make Your Squabbles Proportional.* Minor differences are acknowledged, dismissed, and overlooked in love. Reserve big fights for serious things (Tim and Joy Downs in *Fighting Fair*).
- *Make Empathy a Priority.* As we attempt to understand each other better and develop greater intimacy, we prioritize empathy. Empathy notices, feels, and acts to help each other.
- *Don't Drown Out When They Speak Out.* Refuse to short-circuit the process by skipping over their feelings and trying to make things better or fix things. Don't start too soon.

FOURTH GEAR: RITUALS OF WELCOMES AND GOODBYES

The final gear for making connections is the rituals and routines we use daily to build a rhythm in our relationships. Remember, it's small steps that create giant changes. Over time, routines and rituals lay down grooves in the gears of our relationship. We can either learn to shift smoothly, or we will grind our gears in adverse ways. In *The*

Art and Science of Love, John Gottman says, "A ritual of connection is a method of turning towards one another that is reliable and can be counted on."

Teachers at our local high school model this kind of connection when their students share highs and lows at the beginning of every class period. We do weekly staff meetings at our church where we share grins and wins, and then ask about missing, wrong, or confusing things. These are rituals that are planned out and initiated consistently. Proverbs 11:17 says:

> Those who are kind benefit themselves,
> but the cruel bring ruin on themselves.
> PROVERBS 11:17 NIV

Kindness stimulates mutual empowerment. Cruelty creates chaos. Much conflict occurs when a spouse feels controlled or blamed in a situation or when a mate feels neglected. A spouse who feels controlled will build up resentment. The partner who perceives neglect generates an attitude that their mate is not as invested in the relationship as they are. Nancy will articulate that she often becomes defensive because her perception is that I can be critical and controlling. Yep. On the other hand, my complaint is that sometimes I feel forgotten and ignored. She tells me she will get back to me on that (*wink*).

Dismissive attitudes produce a lack of civility or respect. We stiff-arm kindness and embrace actions that make our spouse feel an inch tall. Contempt is contagious and dangerous. The antidote to contempt is appreciation and gentleness. We can choose the mindset we use. Negative assumptions can be erased, and positive perceptions can be embraced. Perceptions that are used positively have the power to bring transformation.

The Parrots in *The Good Fight* tell the story of Johnny Lingo, who lived in the South Pacific. The dowry he paid for his bride was considered extravagant because she was perceived as plain, skinny, timid, shy, and unattractive. He offered ten cows for his wife when the usual dowry was three. The woman blossomed into a confident, poised, articulate, and rare beauty because she now considered herself worth more than any woman on the islands. Johnny Lingo thought he hit the jackpot and treated his wife like she was the best wife on the planet. She was a ten-cow woman. Kindness elevates. Kindness resonates. Kindness facilitates. Kindness creates.

HELLOS AND GOODBYES

Do you remember the movie *Hitch*, which was filmed before Will Smith was slapping Oscar hosts? Hitch, the date doctor, coaches Albert (Kevin James) to kiss Allegra Cole (Amber Valletta) and reminds him she could have her last first kiss tomorrow night. Hitch instructs Albert on the first kiss to go 90% in and wait for the magic. The teaching moment was not charmed, as Albert was over-eager and laid a smacker right on the date doctor.

I didn't hire a date doctor, but I nailed our first kiss on the porch with Nancy, and I also have the dance skills of Albert. Some of us have it all. Moves like Jaggar and lips like his as well.

Rituals and routines include the way we connect daily. The thrill dissipates when we settle into autopilot and don't include some actions we employed when we first fell in love. Passion morphs into yawning. We forget to include the kisses that make our kids hide their eyes and say, "Yuck." Kissing releases a chemical cascade of feel-good hormones. Go ahead and practice. Pucker up. Lean in 90%. Wait for the magic. Kiss when you leave. Kiss when you arrive. Kiss often and throw in some hugs. And some wet willies. And some noogies. And some well-placed pinches and pats.

The physical gestures we use when saying goodbye and hello to our spouses are some of the most critical components of bids for connections. What brought you together can keep you together. Falling in love is easy. Staying in love is hard. Proverbs 11:25 (NIV) states, "A generous person will prosper; whoever refreshes others will be refreshed." This proverb displays the reciprocal nature of generosity in life.

In *The Art and Science of Love*, John Gottman claims that the recipe for fostering and maintaining a connected and satisfying relationship is investing six hours a week. It includes a ritual where we say goodbye in the morning and learn one thing that will happen in our spouse's life that day. At the end of the day, reunions bring a hug and a kiss that last at least six seconds, accompanied by 20 minutes of stress-reducing conversations. Six seconds is a *lonnnng* smooch. Smooching is aerobic exercise and beats going to the gym.

DATE NIGHTS

Nancy and I have killed a lot of plants. We forget to water hanging baskets, and they fry in a hurry. Nancy now runs bubblers to the baskets so they can blossom. Growing flowers requires thinning weeds and planting seeds. The same is true in marriage. Besides your daily time alone with Jesus to be washed by the Word, nothing sustains a marriage like daily connections with your spouse. Daily union with Jesus doesn't "just happen." Neither does a healthy marriage. Your regular interactions with Jesus and your constant moments in your marriage need divine intervention and your constant attention.

TOUGH TALKS

We need to carve out time on our calendar. We insist. It was part of the commitment we made to one another when I acknowledged I was AWOL physically and emotionally from my wife. Phone calls can wait. Appointments can wait. Schedules can wait. We work hard to refuse to allow schedules to rule our lives. We control our schedules. Time together must be planned. We make time for each other and with each other. This includes meals together and evenings reserved for the relationship, which builds the most essential component of a marriage: friendship.

> The determining factor in whether wives feel satisfied with sex, romance, and passion in their marriage is, by 70 percent, the quality of the couple's friendship.
> For men, the determining factor is, by the same 70 percent, the quality of the couple's friendship.
> So men and women come from the same planet after all.
> Friendship fuels the flames of romance because it offers the best protection against feeling adversarial toward your spouse.
> John Gottman, *The Seven Principles for Making Marriage Work*

"Happily ever after" doesn't happen by chance. It happens with choices. Happiness builds an advantage in our marital, spiritual, physical, emotional, and vocational longevity. We don't want to white-knuckle our way through a long, dry marriage. We want our relationship to blossom. Instead of making them last on a long "to-do" list, we front-load date nights. We deliberately expand our definition of "date night" to include purposeful activity that fits the pattern of our lifestyles.

Marital advisors offer suggestions ranging from weekly extravaganzas to twice-a-week dinners, subscription date boxes, and planned weekend getaways. We know special times happen inconsistently, so we find ways to hang out that work for us, whether we take a long drive or a trip to an Amazon Locker. Don't pressure yourself into disappointment by ejecting before you begin. Start slowly. Find a rhythm. Ask God for wisdom. Surprise your spouse. Play pickleball. Buy a hot dog. Rent an RV.

Play together to stay together. Fun keeps our marriage humming on all cylinders. Couples need time that is face-to-face and side-by-side. Intimacy is not caravanning with your kids to the sports event. Marital health is not sustained sitting beside each other, scrolling through our Instagram or Facebook pages. Date nights are not the time to talk about intense issues or kids' problems. Create planned time together and ditch the kids and other couples. Hanging out doesn't have to be expensive, and couples can be creative in securing childcare.

Choose your marriage as a priority and find regular date nights on a consistent basis. We are empty nesters, so our activities run from Broadway shows to athletic contests. We do musicals and roller coasters. I find roller coasters annoying, but I love my wife. She is worth the upchuck. We ziplined, and she nailed it; I tolerated it.

The instructor told us we could close our eyes and relish the last leg. I told him I hadn't opened my eyes yet. They said to do something funny for a photograph. I picked her up and slipped, and we took a tumble in the dirt. We'll never forget it. We've been told that we would make a good reality series. I'm looking for a producer.

SCHEDULE MARRIAGE HUDDLES

If we never huddle as a couple, we will never leave the line of scrimmage. Huddles are maintenance meetings where we get our play sheet out and get on the same page. Nancy and I talk about everything. We do this informally to ensure our weeks are coordinated and all our bases are covered.

This is also a perfect time to share minor irritations and verbalize appreciation from the recent past. Huddles are regular moments of connection to plan the plays we hope to use in the coming days, and the interactions help remind each other of what's essential and what's trivial.

Another huddle we practice maintaining rhythm in our marriage is to stop working, wanting, and worrying for one day out of seven, called the Sabbath. Our Sabbath is on Monday because Sunday is occupied as a pastor. Sabbath is when we enjoy God and one another and naps. We don't maintain a formula or a checklist except for a reminder that "the seventh day is a sabbath to the LORD your God" (Exodus 20:10a [NIV]). God rested. God delighted. God stopped. We should too. American pastor and writer John Mark Comer echoes a great line by Walter Brueggemann:

> People who keep Sabbath
> live all seven days differently.
> John Mark Comer, *The Ruthless Elimination of Hurry*

It's a simple rhythm rooted in creation. Six and one. I have no sick beat, but I've learned to breathe in this pace to energize our souls and our marriage. It's the unforced tempo of grace.

Another way we bring routines and rhythm is to annually plan a film review on where our marriage is scoring touchdowns and where we are way out of bounds. It's crucial that each spouse knows the agenda and the reason for the getaway (I speak from experience. Don't assume). This time of assessment entails everything from marriage conferences to intentional counseling to finding a way to dream together during a weekend away.

It may seem like overkill, but I've watched marriages implode and erode because of inertia and fear way too often. We talk about our spiritual lives and how we are doing. We discuss our communication styles and how we handle conflict. We renew our covenant commitment and consider how our sexual activity reflects the one-flesh unity God wants to create. We discuss what is going smoothly and where we are missing the mark. Nothing is off limits: money, parenting, legacy, goals, and fun.

A MARITAL MAKEOVER

HGTV is big on whole-home makeovers. We are "all in" on before's and after's. Our marriage reminds us of the front façade of our house. We hauled away junk. We weeded out pesky thistles. We filled the flowerbeds with decorative rocks that required low maintenance. We planted big, beautiful crepe myrtles that are the talk of the neighborhood. We installed decorative lights to highlight the paths. We painted the brick with fresh coats of paint. We wrapped our front posts in cedar.

It's the same house, but it's been transformed. It took a lot of hard work, plenty of time, and some financial investment, but our driveway makeover looks sweet. When I pull in the driveway to park at the end of the day, it's hard to believe it's the same entrance.

Our marriage has entered a different phase as well. We've wrapped our hearts with compassion, coated our attitudes with grace, and highlighted the paths in our marriage with the light of God's truth. We pulled out some tools called "love handles" to break down emotional walls and rebuild stronger foundations. It's been a lot of hard work, a massive emotional investment, and a ton of overcoming.

The hard days aren't all behind us. We still struggle. We push each other's buttons. We fail to make a bid for connection. We miscommunicate and misfire. But we repair the rifts much quicker. We find solid ground at a more rapid pace. We aren't what we need to be. We aren't what we are going to be. Thank God we are not what we used to be. Our marriage is transforming. We are changing into better versions of ourselves.

Next to our front porch is a small concrete slab engraved with our names. It's a marker inscribed with the date our marriage began. At night, an accent light highlights the image. God is engraving something more profound in our marriage. His grace leaves permanent marks. His truth creates imprints.

We aren't making the marriage. The marriage is making us. We aren't perfect, but we are being perfected. Jesus is at the finish line, cheering us on. We hear His voice saying, "Keep running. Keep believing. Keep living. Keep loving." The accent light of our marriage is highlighting the hero of our story. It's not us. It's Jesus.

He started our story, and He will finish it. He will be with us until we take our final breath. We didn't do it. Jesus did. It's the story of our marriage and the story of our lives.

Chapter 5

Recipes and Roots

Nancy and I began a fun tradition as a part of our travel adventures: We attempt to find a unique ornament to hang on one of the 7,329 trees we decorate for Christmas.

Warning, that's a slight exaggeration. We have collected enough ornaments to decorate the National Christmas Tree. Okay, I kid; I kid. The unique pieces chosen from each destination are hung from branches and bring incredible memories of laughing on a crosswalk, kissing on a park bench, reeling in a walleye, feeding a giraffe, or connecting with God in a secluded chapel. The recollections hang from a branch for a couple of months (the number of months gets increasingly longer every year) and then are packed away to reemerge next Christmas. The memories don't disappear; they are stored away for next year.

There are crueler memories stored away that we want to erase, but they resurface more often than every December. We usually don't pull them out in public to display under bright lights; these personal hurts are packed in dark places and hidden away. They hide out in the scarred corners of our souls. Unfortunately, these painful encounters cannot be edited from our marriages and replaced with substitute sentiments. These aren't ornaments; they were initially used as armaments.

- Hateful disputes
- Wounding words
- Toxic texts
- Violation
- Accusation
- Incrimination
- Invalidation
- Disloyalty
- Treachery
- Acrimony

The officiant at our wedding never warned us how much spouses can slay and filet one another. There were no courses we could enroll in to teach us how to handle the damage done by what we said and what we did. We weren't given a heads-up on how to deal with the stranglehold hurt has on our hearts. Instead, we were equipped with a package of decorative declarations handed out to convince everyone and ourselves that we were ok. I call it over-spiritualizing. It's like singing with a falsetto because our real voice doesn't work.

We belt out a multitude of lyrics like:

- "Forgive and forget; it's in the Bible."
- "Build a bridge and get over it."
- "Move on."
- "The past is the past."

- "It is what it is."
- "Others have it worse."

I've sung all those numbers in our marriage. A happy face doesn't heal a hurting space. Burying your pain will only allow it to come out of the dark and bark at the most inopportune times: on a marriage retreat, in a mountain hideaway, after church, on the way to church, in the living room, the bathroom, the bedroom, or at the kitchen table.

Many couples continually nibble on acrimony and live with the aftertaste. We rehearse the wrongs, keep score, pull out our list, and choose confrontation over reconciliation. We stew over the crimes, stir our emotions, and allow them to bake into bitterness. I promise you, bitterness doesn't taste like Pop-Tarts. The more we allow resentment to be baked into our souls, the greater hostility will take over our lives. The trouble is that the people we love the most get to eat what we serve.

Unfortunately, Nancy and I became experts in bedroom brawls and personal throwdowns for a long season in our marriage. Mixed martial arts had nothing over us. We had all the moves down to an art. One classic was back-to-back with a shoulder roll that yanked off the covers. This move was executed with rolling eyes and loud sighs. We had our signature lines used in the square circle of our king-sized bed.

- "Can you hear what I'm saying?"
- "Well, that's obvious."
- "Why do I have to be the bad guy?"
- "That's dumb."
- "I'm sleeping on the couch."

NOTE: These phrases are edited for public broadcast.

What we didn't know when we were looking at our marriage through the lens of puppy love is how often we would be offended. We didn't realize puppy love grows up to bite. In her book, *Forgiving What You Can't Forget: Discover How to Move On, Make Peace with Painful Memories, and Create a Life That is Beautiful Again,* Lysa Terkeurst explains that vulnerability in marriage can facilitate safety or cruelty.

Vulnerability invites, but it also indicts. Openness is an invitation, but it can morph into an accusation. Crushes can crush. Lovers can injure. So, each spouse has a choice to make. *Offense is inescapable, but the decision to live offended is optional.*

We don't have to allow bitterness to be baked into our hearts or resentment to be reheated every time we encounter a past hurt. We can regulate the temperature of the emotions we are cooking.

Here's a public service announcement (don't you love those!) We rarely acknowledge that bitterness is even on the menu. We give it gussied-up names to hide the harm. Restaurants do this with desserts to hide the calories: Paradise Pie, Molten Lava, Chocolate Dream, Cheesecake Bites, and Mini Churros.

Offense wears many disguises that hide the harm and the hurt: sarcasm, overenthusiasm, defensiveness, pensiveness, cynicism, criticism, anxiety, negativity, frustration, or desperation. In our marriages, we dish out revenge in callous stares and icy responses when we refuse to deal with the underlying hurt. No one wants that served up cold.

There's a real danger if we refuse to bring offenses out in the open and call them what they are. What's baked in eventually solidifies. The heart that hardens isn't in a better place, but allows emotional pack rats to nest in the soul. The pack rats pull pieces of memories from distant corners of our memories to carve out a heap of harm. Bitterness blocks grace and the goodness of God. We chew on offenses long enough, and they will create deep heartburn in our marriage. Resentment is reflux. Bitterness leaves a permanent aftertaste.

It takes humility to try a new recipe. God's divine recipe doesn't exclude past ingredients. Still, it does recognize that God can blend the painful and the beautiful into something useful. We are amazed in our marriage how God is the Cake Boss who can take our messes and make a marital work of art. God works His hands in the dough of our hardened hearts to bring out hidden flavors we never saw coming. God can sift the feelings of resentment and bitterness and whisk the healing touch of His forgiveness and compassion into the batter. What God is serving is the love the world craves and the grace we all need.

A BIBLICAL RECIPE FOR RECONCILIATION

There is an art and a science to the recipes used to create a food feast. We've all watched our moms and grandmothers cook with a smidgen of this and a pinch of that while preparing for Thanksgiving. That process is hard to measure and difficult to replicate.

Some of what makes our marriages successful is as unique and mysterious as how our grandmothers prepared a meringue on a coconut crème pie. It's indescribable, but you know what it looks and tastes like. Each God-graced marriage is extraordinary and supernatural, and there's no exact formula for what every marriage needs to find the right blend.

Still, there are biblical steps every couple can follow, as laid out in the written Word, to bring life to any marriage. Two key ingredients are necessary when we are offended: apology and forgiveness. Neither of these is easy. Both are a process to follow and a decision to make. We often verbalize an apology with sincerity, only to have the incident rear its head repeatedly. I grasp what Lysa Terkeurst says in *Forgiving What You Can't Forget*.

> Hurt feelings sometimes don't want to cooperate with holy instructions . . . You make the decision to forgive the facts of what happened. But then you must also walk through the process of forgiveness for the impact those facts have had on you.
> Lysa Terkeurst

We don't *feel* our way to forgiveness or confessions. We cooperate with Jesus to *will* our way to forgiveness. We take a step toward healing only to be ambushed again and again by the intensity of the offense and the bile of bitterness. The process is rarely one-and-done, but the breach does not have to hold us hostage or prevent us from constantly stepping into God's provision of grace.

TRUTH AND GRACE

Our attempts at engaging in the process of the give and take of marital forgiveness don't minimize wrongdoing and pretend that everything is fine. Love isn't evasive and is motivated to take sacrificial steps to tackle the underlying issue. Confrontation and pardon are equally necessary in marriage. Jesus fully embodies truth and grace and calls us to a similar balance in relational rifts. John 1:14 says:

> [Jesus] came from the Father, full of grace and truth.
> JOHN 1:14 NIV [Emphasis Added]

Truth brings an issue to the surface, while grace tries to smooth the resulting waves. Spouses who traffic in truth must temper facts with grace. At the same time, the other partner invites challenging issues to merge into the mercy lane.

It's been our experience in dealing with couples that one spouse leans more into meeting the issue head-on rather than using finesse, while the other favors polish over problem-solving. Often, one spouse is more prone to confront than offer forbearance, and the other is more disposed to forgive but refuses to tackle the issue. In a sense, this is a hollow truth and feigned grace. Hollow truth has a cavity that grace should occupy.

Feigned grace buries the offense through avoidance. Couples devoted to employing truth and grace reveal a commitment to tackling the issue and offering forgiveness. Grace says you can do nothing to make God love you less. Truth tells us there is a remedy, even though we are more sinful than we ever admit. Truth and grace are necessary, according to Jesus in Luke 17:3-4:

> So watch yourselves. If your brother or sister sins against you, rebuke them; and if they repent, forgive them. Even if they sin against you seven times in a day and seven times come back to you saying 'I repent,' you must forgive them.
> LUKE 17:3-4 NIV

Timothy Keller explains in *Forgive: Why I Should and How Can I?* that two actions are set forth here. Loving confrontation and gracious forgiveness are necessary for the restoration of the relationship. This doesn't mean spouses wait to offer forgiveness only when repentance is made and restitution is paid. The quote on the following page tells us that Mark 11:25 says:

> And when you stand praying, if you hold anything against anyone, forgive them, so that your Father in heaven may forgive you your sins.
> MARK 11:25 NIV

This emphatically states that we must forgive if we have anything against anyone. One posture is an inward, emotional decision, while the flip side is an outward, relational process.

In a sense, there are two stages in forgiveness. The first happens inwardly as inner release occurs with the hope of relational repair. Still, reconciliation happens only if both partners take part. This helps us sort some matters out—forgiveness is a choice and a process. I choose to forgive and hope for relational repair.

Forgiveness establishes a foundation for building the restoration of trust. The deeper the damage, the more difficult the rebuilding process becomes. There are circumstances like abuse and infidelity, where violated trust must build boundaries that may prevent a restored relationship. Wisdom and outside guidance are often needed to discern when restoration cannot occur.

100% MY CHOICE

Nancy and I have been involved in vocational pastoral ministry for 38 years. Much as with marriage, we entered the pastorate with high expectations and little realization of how many sinners entered marriage and went to church. I know that's naïve, but please cut a little slack for a wide-eyed idealist.

Of those thirty-eight years, 35 years of ministry were unbelievably rewarding. Three years were like listening to a Creed concert on a loop. I was treated like a piñata on Cinco De Mayo, and rather than spewing out candy, I stored up bitterness. I'm an emotional eater, so

I ate everything in sight. That hostility wasn't the only thing that was swelling. I ate Pringles, Twinkies, Oreos, and Yo-Yos (the candy *and* toy), and compact cars like a Prius. I could have been a Sumo wrestler if I had kept going.

One particular Sunday, the offense spilled out. A terse and ugly email the night before triggered a meltdown. What was happening in secret was revealed from the pulpit in a public breakdown. I should have been madder than hell (still wondering if my wife will let me leave in this phrase), but that's discouraged in pastoral ministry, so I channeled my inner toddler and cratered at the altar. It seemed like the worst moment in my life, but I was about to start the process of becoming a better me.

I stopped lying to myself, trying to make my prayers palatable to God, and started finding my way with Jesus. I didn't have to know why God allowed the pain, or why some decided to traffic in misery and cruelty. I had one choice to make, one step to take, and one life at stake. I had to let the grudges go, leave the bitterness behind, and put the resentment in my rearview mirror. It was my choice to forgive and move forward. We will inevitably be offended, but it's optional for us to stay that way.

Nancy was livid and supportive, and besides Jesus, my greatest ally. I was so distraught. I suggested camping with Nancy in a tent. That's how far gone I was—three straight days on a mountain without a restroom or a shower. Only Creed was worse. Camping helped me unpack some of the stuff stirring in my soul. I decided to pull out the offenses and burn them on the campfire with the s'mores. S'mores taste better, but hurt burns hotter. I know that holding on to offenses in both marriage and ministry prevents relational and personal health.

Was it my choice? 100%. It always is. Forgiving offenses doesn't depend on other people or better circumstances. It's entirely on me. Read Romans 12:18:

> If possible, so far as it depends on you,
> live peaceably with all.
> ROMANS 12:18 ESV

Scripture declares emphatically, "So far as it depends on [me]" [emphasis added]. Peace is my choice. Hope is my choice. Breathing life is my choice. I choose whether I harness my heart to hate or hope. I choose whether I allow hurt to hold my heart hostage. When I decide to continue to allow bitterness to barrage me and cynicism to kidnap me, it's not just me that's getting harmed. It's everyone in my circle.

CONNECT THE DOTS

Everyone in your circle is impacted. That's the takeaway. That's the bottom line. That's the truth to remember. Bitterness isn't usually visible to the naked eye, but it is seen in the sphere around us. Bitter roots spread to touch everyone close to us. Our spouses are first. The kids aren't spared. Our circle of friends is in the well of contamination. The roots don't stop growing.

Rancorous roots are like the invasive zebra mussels in the Great Lakes. I love repeating this story because I caught a large walleye in Pelican Lake in Minnesota. It was our one and only time to use a fishing guide. He filled us in on the invasive, fingernail-sized mollusk with dark, zig-zagged stripes on each shell. These mollusks adhere like superglue to anything and everything they touch, clogging up power plants and boat propellers.

Our fishing guide explained the stringent steps to prevent species from continuing to taint everything the mussels touch. Each boat and trailer is inspected before being allowed back into the lake. Every boat must be washed and drained after contact and then dried in the sun for five days. Imagine what kind of relational revival might occur if marriage partners took even a fraction of the steps to prevent bitterness from building up in their relationships:

> Make every effort to live in peace with everyone and to be holy; without holiness no one will see the Lord. See to it that no one falls short of the grace of God and that no bitter root grows up to cause trouble and defile many.
> HEBREWS 12:14-15 NIV

Such bitter roots have long tentacles and poisonous touches and cause trouble in double doses. The pollution of the poison infects other people by pumping venom into their veins. Bitterness never stays private; it always finds a way to go public. Toxic texts look for any platform to spread the hurt. Social media has the seeds of bitterness spreading to every nook and cranny. We can't open our apps without drinking the Kool-Aid. Bitterness spreads its tentacles throughout our terrain.

It's why the command is continuous: "Make every effort to live in peace with everyone and to be holy." *Everyone* includes the one you promised to love from this day forward. *Everyone* includes our enemies. The biblical instruction doesn't allow us to opt out because of extenuating circumstances or exempt us because we live with a difficult person. *Everyone* is inclusive and doesn't allow us to carve people out of the command. Are we attempting to live in peace with the one across from us? Do we realize that to live at peace with others, we've got to unleash the peace that Jesus offers us?

This effort to live in harmony with everyone isn't passive reluctance but active resistance. We must stand up and fight for peace. It's ironic that in marriage, we wage war for harmony. We go to the mat for our marriage and our mate. We strive and struggle and wrestle and grapple to maintain marital goodwill. We fight an ancient foe who hates how marriage mirrors the mystery of how much Jesus loved the church and gave Himself up for her. Why did Jesus do this?

> To make her holy, cleansing her by the washing with water through the word, and to present her to himself as a radiant church, without spot or wrinkle or any other blemish, but holy and blameless.
> EPHESIANS 5:26-27 NIV

These verses include a destination and reservations for a couple wanting to mirror the Messiah. The book of Ephesians mandates that husbands echo Jesus as they present their wives as radiant brides. Show her who she is becoming instead of pointing to her blemishes. Point out her potential instead of her flaws.

The quest for marital sanctity will lead to relational harmony. Husbands decide how they present their wives and represent their Savior. Constant criticism doesn't create marital unity, and disdain and contempt are far from demonstrating holiness. We can allow our marriage to illustrate the profound mystery between Christ and the church (Ephesians 5:32).

Take a moment to connect the dots from the passages in Ephesians and Hebrews. How many of us did that activity in grade school? We grab our pencils and follow the numbers, and a picture emerges. In elementary school, the sketch that appeared might be an image of a disappearing species, like a dinosaur or a platypus. Similarly, the dots God asks us to connect in marriage are now in danger of extinction.

Marriage is increasingly frowned upon as an obsolete institution that many circles don't honor or value. *Holy* is an uncommon label in our culture that few people stick to in their lives. It is perceived as an outdated notion with little validity in the 21st century. Peace is viewed as an abstract principle with little relevance in day-to-day affairs.

The command to be holy and live peaceably is a dual quest that only a few pursue. An exceptional marriage means we follow a particular path that the masses miss. It's not dismissing ordinary because much of what we do is mundane, where a marriage is made. But every marriage needs to aim for the extraordinary. The road is narrow, and a small subset finds the lane that leads to healthy destinations in the marital journey.

Consider the questions John Mark Comer asks in *Loveology: God. Love. Marriage. Sex. And the Never-Ending Story of Male and Female.*

- Will you live set apart?
- Will you commit your marriage to spiritual flourishing?
- Will you connect the dots of living peaceably and becoming holy to create marital harmony?

These are penetrating questions that lead to a tough decision. As a pastor, I see constant examples of those who live outside the lines of God's boundaries and the chaos that ensues. Spouses mimic TikTok trends and Instagram influencers, which leads to predictable outcomes. God's way isn't ordinary or easy; in fact, it's the road much less traveled. Why not do what others avoid to discover what others miss? Why not ignore the usual and shoot for the incomparable?

Peace prevents coming apart. Peace is saying no to good things to find better things, like life with God and one another. Holy sets us apart from the ordinary to pursue something special. Holy does something different to find something excellent. Trek both paths, and they merge in a surprisingly special and remarkably flourishing marriage: becoming holy and living in peace. Anybody can do ordinary. Only God empowers unmatched glory. We would rather aim for a masterpiece highlighted in a museum than a mass-produced print hung in a motel.

The painting that develops looks like our Savior. Hebrews says holiness is the only way we ever see the Lord. Hebrews also says the only way we become holy is through the perfect sacrifice of our Savior. Hebrews 10:14 (NIV) says:

> For by one sacrifice he has made perfect
> forever those who are being made holy.
> **HEBREWS 10:14 NIV**

We pursue what we've already been given: peace in full measure and the confidence we can enter God's presence because of the holiness of His Son. We should actively and eagerly pursue peace, and constantly and diligently endeavor to be holy.

> But just as he who called you is holy,
> so be holy in all you do;
> for it is written: "Be holy, because I am holy."
> **1 PETER 1:15-16 NIV**

> Whoever would love life and see good days
> must keep their tongue from evil
> and their lips from deceitful speech.
> They must turn from evil and do good;
> they must seek peace and pursue it.
> 1 PETER 3:10-11 NIV

Holiness isn't haughtiness but surrendering to become more and more like God's Son. That's the path to His presence. It's less of us and more of Him. It's not image management. Instead, it's upper management remaking us in His image. We didn't negotiate a settlement; Jesus canceled the charges against us by a once-and-for-all transaction where He paid the price we could never pay and forgave all our sins. He was nailed to the cross so that He could nail our condemnation to the cross. His provision is the only way we will ever see the Lord.

We don't make ourselves better and improved; instead, we give ourselves to the One who presents us as brand new. The Holy One was stained by sin, so those stained by sin could be made holy. We don't make ourselves right, but unrighteous sinners find that in Jesus, we are made right with God.

Forgiveness is a decision and a process, which means there is a giving and receiving in marriage that must be accepted. If a spotless, sinless Savior through His once-and-for-all sacrifice on a cross could reconcile us to a holy God, we can be reconciled to one another. God's forgiveness came because we confessed to Him, "You are holy and right. I am sinful and wrong. I ask for Your forgiveness."

We must abandon our rightness and uprightness to discover that Jesus is our righteousness. The pardon of our Savior gives us a model to adopt as we seek reconciliation. His pardon emboldens statements like these: "I am sorry. I was wrong. I messed up." Hebrews 12:15 implores us:

> See to it that no one falls short of the grace of God.
> **HEBREWS 12:15a NIV**

Anytime we grudgingly view God's grace, we abandon ourselves to the outcome of bitterness that defiles many and causes trouble. Don't forfeit this opportunity and fall short of the grace God offers. Don't come to forgiveness reluctantly, but willingly. Kneel at the cross and marvel at His grace. Recognize that because Jesus did this for us, we must extend it to the one closest to us.

Connect the dots. The Truth is recognizable, and grace is available. Take both in large doses, and you will find a path to peace and the hope of holiness.

Chapter 6

Apologies and Mirrors

I've been a pastor for thirty-eight years and get paid to be the good guy. Pastoring is a deterrent to sinful behavior and an accelerant for doing the right thing. Much of this concerns reputation and guarding how things appear. Almost anyone can shake hands, smile, nod, and even memorize a script to repeat.

The problem is the criterion given in passages like Titus 1:7. Pastors are to "not be overbearing or quick-tempered" for starters, and "blameless" for an overarching ambition. I can do that for a few hours or even several days. But it quickly unravels in a familiar place: when I enter the front door of my home. There, I take off my shoes and status and become the real me.

Every day, I go home to a full-length mirror given to me on my wedding day: my spouse. Now, we often want to put our spouse in front of a mirror and ask God to fix them. In reality, God gave us a mirror in our spouses, which fully reveals the uncorrected versions of ourselves. No one has unearthed the real Joe Stewart more than

Nancy. I get the unvarnished version of my wife as well. Marriage is merciless about revealing the harsh facts. It's like vanity lights in the bathroom: they can make us look unpleasant because they uncover all the blemishes. We either dim the lights, avoid the mirror, or repair the reflection. Vanity and pretense in a marriage leave us with a reputation but little reality.

The challenging work of vulnerability requires long looks at ourselves, making shifts that hone us. No honest participant is without wrinkles or blemishes. Still, God can use our marriage to fashion apologies that lead to lasting change. Such apologies can mend broken hearts and build bridges across relational chasms.

THE ART OF THE APOLOGY

Marriage enrolls us in an advanced class in crafting an apology. If marriage isn't enough, sprinkle in some kids. It's why the word *diaper* spelled backward is *repaid*. Marriage and parenting give us innumerable opportunities to say we are sorry. Why, then, are apologies so stinking hard?

If you are old enough to remember, many of us are Fonzie when it comes to saying we are sorry. (He was a character in the television series, *Happy Days*, and struggled to even utter the phrase "I was wrong.") We are hooked on being right and often take a "deny and defend" stance. They tick us off, so we write them off. Apologizing is hard because it requires humility, which is important as it builds sincerity and transparency. I hate to break it to the masses, but despite our best aims and intent, it is unavoidable.

At some point in our marriages and parenting, we will be wrong. I know it feels fabulous to stick to our guns, and the refusal to apologize can create momentary relief. But digging in our heels will eventually give us sore feet and tired backs. According to one author, saying "I'm sorry" involves admitting "I am wrong," which requires disclosing errors and restoring trust. Love necessitates each partner learning to say they're sorry well. It requires a twofold practice of saying things sincerely and using specificity. Continuing refusals to apologize can create distance in marriage and morph minor disagreements into long-standing disharmony. Unrepaired or inadequately addressed injuries lead to erosion in the relationship and the escalation of defensive responses from our partners. Molly Howes states it well:

> Over time, such arguments become automatic, like the "muscle memory" of actions you can do with your eyes closed.
> Molly Howes

Resolving hurt and misunderstanding unwinds habitual negative routines to help facilitate a better path forward with improved feelings about future challenges. Such a posture of facing challenges will not rectify every issue, but no issue can be resolved unless it is faced.

Making the first move is hard. Let me repeat a phrase from a previous chapter: *Awkward* is better than avoidance. I'm a chronic procrastinator in going first with an apology. I know I can be as stubborn as our barking dog, Lucy, when she sees movement at the front door. We don't need a notification from our Ring doorbell app when Lucy surveys the street.

The slightest motion brings a quick yelp. No matter how much correction or soothing is offered, she continues to bark. Sometimes, it's under her breath. That describes the approach many of us take in initiating dialogues about difficult topics. *We'd rather yap inside our heads than tackle a challenging conversation.*

I'm often trapped in my brain when it comes to owning up to a regret in word or action with Nancy. Often, I'd rather stay stuck in the muck, nursing my hurt, rather than notice any way I might have wounded my wife. In my internal thoughts, I argue that I should wait for her to come to her senses because her logic is skewed. I reinforce this concept with all the occasions she messed up before.

Such a stance prevents an apology and keeps the ball in Nancy's court, where I assume it belongs. I realize that stating my mental stances seems like self-justification. Still, perhaps, just perhaps, we all do a smidgen of this. (Do you sense the snark?)

This is where an apology comes in. An apology expresses regret: "I am sorry." A confession admits fault: "I am sorry because I did wrong." Confession brings peace inside me. An apology creates peace around me. Confession is inward. An apology is outward. It matters how we say we are sorry. It's impossible to genuinely say the words, "I'm sorry," without swallowing our own pride.

The problem is we often choke before we get the words out, and what we offer is an excuse instead of an admission. It's Splenda instead of sugar as a low-calorie, pride-preserving substitute for the genuine article. Here are some classic examples of pseudo-apologies listed from *Fight Fair* by Tim and Joy Downs:

PSEUDO-APOLOGIES

- Apology without remorse: "Logically, I'll admit you have a point."
- Premature apology: "I'm sorry, I'm sorry; now, can we drop the whole thing?"
- Apology of expedience: "All right, I'm sorry; now, can we watch the game?"
- Angry Apology: "Ok! I'm sorry! Is that what you wanted?"

- Excusing Apology: "I'm sorry, but . . . ."
- Absence of Malice Apology: "I'm sorry, but I wasn't trying to hurt you."
- Minimizing Apology: "I'm sorry you feel bad."
- Misstated Apology: "I'm sorry I said it that way."
- Partial Apology: "I was just kidding."
- The Get-Off-My-Back Apology: "Enough already, I am sorry, alright?"
- The Others-Have-It-Worse Apology: "I'm sorry, but there are a lot of people who have it worse than we do."
- No Responsibility Apology: "I'm sorry this whole thing happened."
- Bitter Apology: "I'm sorry for everything. Look at what you made me do."
- Evasive Apology: "Let's not be mad anymore."
- Cease-fire Apology: "I'm willing to call a truce if you are."
- Burial Apology: "Let's just forget the whole thing."
- Perspective Apology: "We've got more important things to worry about than this."
- You are Unreasonable Apology: "I'm sorry, I'm not perfect."
- Blame-shifting Apology: "I'm sorry you're so sensitive."
- Blame-sharing Apology: "I guess we really blew it, didn't we?"
- Self-deprecating Apology: "I don't know why you ever married me."
- Trivializing Apology: "Hey, it's no big deal. Sorry."

ACCIDENTAL BUMPS

These phrases often use the words "I'm sorry" but never apologize at all. There's no ownership, remorse, or responsibility for what you said or did. It's a non-admission disclosure. The biblical word for an apology is repentance. This is essential to relational health and maintaining an accurate view of our marriage. Repentance toward our mate is formed as an apology and is something every spouse should excel in offering. At this point, we learn to stifle apologies with a few defense mechanisms to prevent genuine connection: stonewalling, contempt, criticism, and defensiveness.

Too often, we aren't engaged in repairing marital rifts as much as we are positioning ourselves to stand our ground and guard our position. It's interesting how I escalate matters, and Nancy is prone to withdraw. Sometimes, we switch scenarios, but neither viewpoint leads to healthy interactions. Neither stance is a posture of listening. Listening requires a receptive attitude and a decision to ask for a genuine reaction to the damage done. I know I'm guilty of assuming I already know how my wife feels without hearing her say it out loud.

Sometimes, even unintentional slights or bumps are more complicated than we realize. As an elementary boy, I accidentally bumped into a man in a hardware store. I had entered the store with my family and quickly wandered off, as I am prone to do. I was oblivious to people around me and accidentally jolted a stranger, followed by an offhanded, "Oops, I'm so sorry."

What I wasn't expecting was how quickly the situation spiraled into a crisis. I didn't mean to do anything wrong, but the tightly close aisles led to a tense scenario. My dad intervened and helped rectify the harm. However, I still remember the incident as if it had happened six seconds ago.

This happens in marriage as we inhabit close quarters, and unintended hurts happen. We can leave marks on our mate, even inadvertently, as we tread into sensitive places. We can step on our spouse's emotional toes without realizing what we've done. We often hope a quick "Oops, I'm so sorry" will repair the rift. But many times, uncomfortable conversations need to happen before apologies can occur. It will take time and effort to get it "right," and it won't happen immediately. But leaning in and listening to understand is a step in the right direction.

Too often, we go backward and become defensive. Defensiveness is a natural reaction, like putting up a glove when a line drive is headed your way in baseball. Or ducking when your spouse playfully hurls a pair of socks at your head. This initial reaction is expected, but what we do next facilitates an actual apology. After hearing the initial comment offered by our spouse and receiving the opening bid for connection, we need to take time. Time to sort out our thoughts and think through our reactions. Rather than accelerate or escalate with a quick retort, we can listen attentively to the shared hurt.

These methods of listening attentively aren't automatic responses but ways of communication that must be repeated and practiced. Habits die hard, and as we are asked to listen long and speak short, it's easier said than done. Anger accelerates words from a comment into a speech, a speech into a sermon, and a sermon into a series.

Apologies are about more than words, and "I'm sorry" isn't magic fairy dust that makes things go away. We can't talk our way out of a situation we behaved our way into. We must behave our way out of it. We teach our children these patterns when we ask them to do more than say they are sorry. Since we practice this with our kids, we can rehearse the steps with one another. It may mean pausing, taking a break, and then backtracking to rehear.

Apologies require the hearer to put aside personal grievances and established ideas of what happened. They help us release defined expectations of how our mate should respond. Instead, active listening minimizes interruptions, short-circuits personal attempts at justification, and curtails comments to diminish the complaints of our spouse. It avoids statements like: "That's not what I meant." "Why are you bringing that up now?" "I was only doing what I thought you needed." Active listening is tough when we feel unfairly attacked or inaccurately described. The tendency is to quickly mount a counterattack in a defensive response. The key to preventing defensiveness is to stay present, live in the moment, and attempt to pick up the cues we missed.

Suppose defensiveness is ramping up when our spouse mentions an unwanted impact. In that case, stonewalling entails shutting down emotionally in a refusal to establish intimacy. Stonewalling withdraws from our spouses, even if we are in the same room. We do this by avoiding eye contact, crossing our arms, and daring our mate to penetrate our defenses. Evading the issue doesn't create a connection. Such obstruction isn't active listening but passive resistance that turns off healthy interaction.

This barrier prevents asking clarifying questions about what is at the core. A key component in preventing such patterns is to bring God into the equation through prayer. This will defuse our need to justify ourselves and allow God to step in on our behalf.

ESSENTIALS OF AN APOLOGY

What are the elements of an honest confession? How do we exhibit genuine repentance? The essential piece at the core of expressing remorse is to respond appropriately to what is revealed as you listen. It makes listening and understanding so meaningful because now you can honestly say where you missed the mark. This step, in a sense, is where we face the music. It's where we express regret for the hurt we caused, take responsibility for the impact we had, and attempt to remediate the harm we've done.

When taken appropriately in a genuine apology, this step focuses on repairing the rift by owning what we've done. We take responsibility rather than allow a breach by attempting to convince our spouse that we aren't at fault. It's modeling John 1:14:

> The Word became flesh
> and made his dwelling among us.
> We have seen his glory,
> the glory of the one and only Son,
> who came from the Father,
> full of grace and truth.
> JOHN 1:14 NIV

Genuine apologies model grace and truth. Grace says, "I'm for you, as I forgive you no matter what." Truth reveals, "I'm with you, as I'm honest with you, no matter what." One author says, "Truth minus grace is hot sauce that leads to relational meltdowns."

Grace minus truth is weak sauce, which refuses to own up and step up. Grace plus truth is our secret sauce! Apologies use the perfect combination of truth-telling and grace-giving. You combine grace and truth, and relationships flourish.

Experts vary in terminology, but the essentials of meaningful relational repair are recognizable. There are no magic words or wands to wave to create connection, but God promises to give us the words that fit when we need them (Matthew 10:19). The key isn't proper technique but a concerned heart that is determined to heal the rupture in the relationship. Trust is restored as the air is cleared and engagement is made. The essential steps include:

1. *Remorse.* An authentic apology begins with a recognition that we've caused actual harm. It does not minimize the impact or diminish the hurt that is caused. Such an apology maintains empathy and appropriate intensity.

2. *Responsibility.* A sincere apology doesn't shift blame or make excuses for the actions that were taken or the absence of intervention. It avoids words like "if," "but," and "maybe" as it attempts to own the act or failure to act. Jesus taught us to pray, "Forgive us our debts,"—not excuse our missteps. All you can control is your own actions. Make the first move. Take the first step. Jesus said in Matthew 5:23-24:

> Therefore, if you are offering your gift at the altar
> and there remember that your brother or sister
> has something against you,
> leave your gift there in front of the altar.
> First go and be reconciled to them;
> then come and offer your gift.
> MATTHEW 5:23-24 NIV

The altar is in the temple in Jerusalem. The Sermon on the Mount is delivered on the north shore of Galilee. Here's some context. That's 72 miles on foot as the crow flies. Sincere apologies are never convenient or easy, but they are worth the trip.

3. *Repair.* The practice of repentance includes an effort to repair the damage we've caused and create new patterns of living. This part of an apology is realizing that a lack of follow-through shows a lack of repentance. We need to act and alter behaviors to keep the hurt from recurring. Repair includes the words, "Will you forgive me?" and "This is how I intend to change."

Here are some scripts to use in the repair from Tim and Joy Downs' book *Fight Fair*:

- "Here's how I will make sure this never happens again."
- "I want to do whatever I can to earn your trust by refusing to use that language."
- "I promise to take responsibility for changing my routine/habits/mindset."
- "Together, can we figure out a way to change how we communicate in conflict?"
- "Will you please tell me if you see that we're sliding into the old pattern again?"

Zacchaeus showed these values in Luke 19 when salvation came to His house. Jesus arrived as "...the Son of Man...to seek and save the lost," (Luke 19:10b [NIV]). The story implies that Zacchaeus cheated scores of people out of money in his role as a chief tax collector.

His new relationship with the Savior led to remorse for his original stance. He accepted responsibility for the harm he caused and attempted to repair the damage he had done. He pledged to give half of his possessions to the poor and pay back four times the amount to anyone he cheated in collecting taxes. These actions reflect the value of a genuine apology.

The steps to repair a marriage cannot be taken from a distance—they require that we get up close and personal. Suggestions, hints, indirect communication, buying a gift, making dinner, and using humor do nothing to create correction or connection. Remorse is an emotional involvement that tells your spouse you care and are concerned about how the incident caused harm in the relationship.

Genuine sorrow includes contrition and distress about how the relationship was ruptured. An apology begins with a decision, and the choice involves invoking empathy and maintaining appropriate intensity in our apology. There is no one-size-fits-all approach, but a recognition that the energy we employ in our admission needs to reflect the size of the harm we've caused.

Responsibility is not an admission of total fault, but an understanding that every disagreement has two sides. We are not owning what we didn't do, but fessing up to where we acted inappropriately. It might be how we raised our voice or said something sarcastic. It could be that our timing wasn't right, or the tone of our tune was in the wrong key. Responsibility includes the desire to protect our mate and expose the roots of evil so they might be rendered ineffective. Responsibility stops the cycle of offense and embraces the grip of God's grace with profound gratitude for how much God has forgiven us.

Accepting responsibility doesn't mean that all the blame belongs to you; it means that, when it comes to your part, you need to be careful not to pass the buck to someone or something else.

AN APOLOGY SCRIPT

Remedy goes the extra mile to repair the breach that caused the hurt. This is the ethic and example of Jesus. He didn't go halfway in paying the cost to secure our salvation. He went all the way to the cross, where God gave love freely in an infinitely costly way. We are all sinners saved by grace, extending the grace we were given. We are deeply loved and profoundly sinful. The forgiveness of Jesus dealt with both. This is the remedy of transformation that brings the repair of reconciliation. Transformation begins with an apology. An apology is the choice to move forward instead of staying stuck. Here's a script to practice:

- *Acknowledge your need to apologize.* Please recognize that this is ground level and establishes the ability to have future conversations, but it does not include them. Apologies are most effective when they are specific and straightforward.
- *Permission is granted to begin the process.* Ask if this is a good time to start the process. What you are saying is important and deserves the best from each party. Poor timing derails many apologies.
- *Offer two phrases: "I was wrong" and "I am sorry."* Apologies are not about you. You are not here to criticize and blame. Dial down your defensiveness.
- *Listen to respond with empathy and appropriate intensity to the hurt.* Refuse to rush the other person to forgive or request a particular response. Give them time and space to process the request. Persistence and patience are needed.
- *Own your part in the offense.* Keep the lines of communication open without allowing improper boundaries to be crossed. Ask for heavenly wisdom.
- *Go the extra mile.* Establish patterns that keep the offense from being repeated.
- *Yearn for reconciliation.* Forgiveness is both a choice and a process. Don't make the apology dance to a circular firing squad. Move toward greater connection. Over-focusing on yourself and under-focusing on your spouse leads to greater distance.

We often fail to recognize that this apology process doesn't weaken marriage but strengthens our bond. Tim and Joy Downs explain this in *Fight Fair*. The Japanese have developed a process that repairs broken pottery, known as *kintsukuroi*. The cracks that remain after restoring the piece are lined with gold and silver. What emerges in the process is even more beautiful and stronger than the original art form.

The full impact of an apology isn't immediate and takes time to be seen and shine. Relationships must employ the long game to flourish as we cultivate honesty, humility, gentleness, compassion, and forbearance.

We had an ornament on our Christmas tree that was smashed to smithereens years ago by an inadvertent bump of a branch. The ornament said, "First Christmas Together—1980," and was a sentimental piece. It was impossible to glue the pieces back together. But we still placed the ornament's original plastic casing (minus the glass) in the tree as a reminder of where we've been and how far we've come. What remains of the marriage we started in 1980 is only a shell of what we began. Expectations have been shattered, sentiments removed, and a marriage has been rebuilt piece by piece.

We've been broken together. God has taken what slipped from our hands, crashed and smashed on the floor, and made something new. In a sense, God took the slivers and the glitter of our original start and restored the spark and beauty by gluing us together in a different fashion. This is the essence of what it means to live in the unity of one-flesh intimacy.

What we now display reflects how God uses damaged pieces to display His grace and glory. What we broke with obstinate refusals to apologize, God mended by calling us to move with courage. Courage revealed itself as we climbed out on the end of the branch and the breach to move towards reconciliation. These moves allow His light to penetrate the broken shards and glow in ways we never imagined. Every time we hang the plastic casing of the original ornament on our Christmas tree, we marvel at how far we've come and how far we have to go.

The difference is that we now recognize the only way forward is in the hands of our Heavenly Father. He is the master artisan who takes the messes of our marriage and makes a masterpiece by the touch of His grace and the gift of His mercy.

Chapter 7

Forgiveness and Referees

Forgiveness closes the distance between spouses, although forgiveness is usually more challenging than an apology. One of the greatest taglines in cinematic history occurs in the drama of marital infidelity in *The Painted Veil*: "Sometimes the greatest journey is the distance between two people."

This tale of a husband and wife, adapted from a W. Somerset Vaughn novel, narrates the chasm between partners rooted in unrecognized expectations. The implicit difficulty in forgiveness is uncovered by the husband lifting the veil when he states:

> It was silly of us to look for qualities
> in each other that we never had.
> W. Somerset Vaughn

> In marriage, we seldom get the chance to say,
> "I forgive you;" we always have to say,
> "I forgive you again."
> Tim and Joy Downs

DOING THE WORK OF FORGIVENESS

Forgiveness offers the ultimate test when our spouse provides an apology for the umpteenth time. Couples have to put into practice the truth presented when Peter quizzed Jesus, "'Master, how many times do I forgive a brother or sister who hurts me? Seven?' Jesus replied, 'Seven! Hardly. Try seventy times seven,'" (Matthew 18:21b-22 [MSG]). In another gospel, when the disciples were told the "seventy times seven" standard (i.e., open-endedly, always), they exclaimed, "Increase our faith!" (Luke 17:5 [NIV])

Forgiveness is not easily forgetting, but instead thoughtfully processing the offense. Forgiveness is the hard work that says the current state is not okay, and the hassle of dealing with the hurt is worth the investment. Forgiveness is far from forgetfulness, but is a recollection and deep appreciation for the grace given by God for our own personal sin.

Paul David Tripp says the following in his book, *Marriage*:

> Why is it we are so skilled at remembering the other's weakness, failure, and sin and so adept at forgetting our own? Why are we so good at seeing all the ways that another needs to be forgiven, but forget how great our need for forgiveness is? Perhaps a lifestyle of unforgiveness is rooted in the sin of forgetfulness. We forget that there is not a day in our lives that we do not need to be forgiven. We forget we will never graduate from our need for grace. We forget that we have been
> [cont'd next page]

loved with a love we could never earn, achieve, or deserve.
We forget that God never mocks our weakness,
never finds joy in throwing our failures in our face,
never threatens to turn his back on us,
and never makes us buy our way back into his favor.
When you remember,
when you carry with a deep appreciation
for the grace that you have been given,
you'll have a heart that is ready to forgive.
Paul David Tripp

REFEREES AND FORGIVENESS

Some of us think we are always better than average. Just ask me. I can opine on a host of issues. Mullets are strangely alluring. The Oxford comma is the only way to go. Pluto is a planet. The TV series, *The Office,* is cringeworthy. The superiority of seventies music is absolutely unquestionable.

Most of us occupy the seat of armchair quarterbacks, backseat drivers, and Monday morning critics. And we assess ourselves as smarter than the average bear. Go to any sporting event and watch as calls are made in the game by referees, coaches, and players. And there is almost always a vocal minority who will loudly object that they would have made a different (better) call. Our confidence often exceeds our competence in various settings, from the superintendent calling a bad-weather day at school to our President sending troops into harm's way. In this default position, we are working to convince others that we are right and to prove the point that the other side is in the wrong.

Does this sound a lot like marriage? We often serve as pundits, offering our spouse strident statements from our perches while convincing our mate they are way wide of the mark. Too frequently, as marriage partners, we see ourselves as superior to our companions. Any personal mistakes we make are deemed unintentional and out of our control. Conversely, we decide our mate's point of view is an intentional deficiency. This stance refuses to accurately depict how often we are prone to offend our spouses in the moment. Such strokes leave the canvases of our marriages dotted with bad textures and thick residue.

Instead, spouses would do well to paint with brushstrokes thinned by the mixture of humility and wisdom. Humility is concerned with flexibility, while wisdom searches for accuracy. Humility is the ability to assess the situation so that we don't paint with a broad brush and a harsh hand. Wisdom gains a perch to view the snapshot of the circumstances from God's point of view. The apostle Paul put it eloquently.

> Because of the privilege and authority God has given
> me, I give each of you this warning:
> Don't think you are better than you really are.
> Be honest in your evaluation of yourselves,
> measuring yourselves by the faith God has given us.
> ROMANS 12:3 NLT

I used to be more vocal at local athletic contests until I was recruited to put on a striped shirt and referee basketball games. It's farther than you think from the sidelines to the court. The pay is not bad until you factor in irate fans in the stands and the fuming coaches on the sidelines. Criticism is merciless when mascots and cheerleaders join the fray. The scene is comical because, as a pastor, I get paid to yell it like it is. And as a referee, I get paid for others to yell at me. I am expected to calm down and not take it personally.

I quickly learned that referees have different angles when the action is moving fast at floor level. They might see things others miss or miss things that others see. The key to good officiating is consistent calls at both ends of the floor and constant communication of what led to a particular whistle. We all want to get the call right. Too often in officiating, "me" gets in the way of "we" and leads to chaos. Sometimes, what coaches say is out of bounds, needs to be challenged (often by a whistle), and leads to technical fouls and penalties.

The challenge in refereeing is constantly improving and doing your best to let the players determine the outcome. Expert referees learn to stay involved but out of the way and not interfere with the flow of the contest. A final lesson I discovered as a referee is that when I make a boneheaded call, I need to own up to the miscue and not multiply the mistake. These same factors apply in the search for forgiveness in our marriages:

- There are different angles from which to see the offense. We might see things the other partner misses or miss items the other spouse sees.
- Words, actions, gestures, attitudes, body language, and facial expressions move fast. We must cue in and consistently respond to what is being done and said.
- The issue is the issue, not the way the issue is handled. Work to repair the relationship and not get embroiled in disagreement about how we got to a decision.
- Things said that are out of bounds (or below the belt) need to be challenged. We need to remember the boundaries decided beforehand.
- Consistency demands we hold ourselves to the same standard we ask of our spouse.

- Own up to our own violations by acknowledging when we are boneheaded. Clarify when the conflict is misunderstood.
- "Me" can easily get in the way of "We." Couples need to stay engaged without taking things too personally.

CLIMBING THE LADDER OF FORGIVENESS

Forgiveness is a steep climb. It attempts to ascend above the offense, over the anger, and through the hurt to gain distance from the initial event. Jesus modeled a path to forgiveness when He allowed Himself to be deliberately nailed to a cross. This scandalous act was God's way of saying that evil is real and must be conquered. Jesus humbled Himself and died a criminal's death on a cross (Philippians 2:5).

This act of forgiveness was initiated as Jesus refused to cling to divine prerogatives; instead, He scaled down the ladder from heaven to a place of ultimate demotion. Jesus surrendered His rights as He deliberately made Himself nothing. Forgiveness was His choice, and He was not coerced, pushed, or cajoled into the act. Step by deliberate step, Jesus chose to move from the pinnacle of creation to the debasement of the cross. Jesus, in freedom, loved in order to break the chain of evil, because sin is serious and forgiveness is needed. Forgiveness was His great "Yes." Jesus surrendered so that we might be free. This path of forgiveness was His decision to deal with the hand He was dealt.

Everyone is dealt something. I don't say that casually. I've been spared some of the damage many have faced. Still, the human condition doesn't spare anyone from eventually getting a bad draw. It's not luck, but life that brings hurt and heartache in spades. No one knows the hand they will be dealt, but only a rare few get an inside straight. Too many get raw deals: abuse, infidelity, inattention, trauma, and hurt. Jesus pays the ante and doesn't throw anyone on the discard pile.

Marriage, by definition, means you get increased opportunities to play the wrong cards. This means every couple must ascend the ladder of forgiveness, because forgiveness isn't something we feel; forgiveness is something we decide. The choice before us is to do the hard work of loving our neighbor to show our love of God. No neighbor is closer than the spouse beside us, and no act we choose is more restorative than the presence of mercy when an offense occurs. The ground is level at the foot of the cross, and a ladder of forgiveness is planted in its soil.

THE GROUND FLOOR OF FORGIVENESS

Let's acknowledge from the beginning that the choice to enter communion and covenant with our spouse is a choice to love. And the choice to love means we extend grace and forgiveness to a fellow sinner. The apology is on the bottom floor. The ladder is placed on the ground of the offense, and the forgiver scales the rungs to get above the hurt and leave the issue below. The first step is choosing to take the first step.

The footing where the ladder begins must find solid ground, not uneven terrain, because uneven terrain unleashes the crazy train. That's where many of us live in marriage. Rather than climb the ladder, we keep spinning our wheels and digging deeper holes. "Crazy" catches up to us, leading to relational wrecks and scattered emotional debris.

We've boarded the crazy train way too often for way too long. Marriage, over time, comprises more relational detours than most of us could ever imagine. We all carry a host of people with us into the marriage. As Peter Scazzero says in his book, *Emotionally Healthy*

Spirituality, "Jesus may be in my heart, but grandpa is in my bones." Some painful patterns are shared, and marriage quickly unveils what's buried in the marrow.

Many of my reactions in my marriage are rooted in a fear of abandonment. My mom and dad split for a season when I was in the fifth grade, and it left deep scars. The scarring left yawning wounds in my neural networks that colored much of our early years of marriage. Much conflict emerged from an irrational need for connection, leading me to take perceived rejection personally. Often, I would interpret an interruption in connection as an intentional injury that led to boarding the crazy town express.

This pattern created serious problems because I elevated my emotional intensity to levels of insanity in misguided attempts to create intimacy. Intensity doesn't lead to intimacy, but engagement with the underlying emotions can pave the way for a genuine relationship. I'd demand attention so I wouldn't lose connection. That's uneven ground because it leads to guardedness, inauthenticity, and relational chaos. Smoothing the ground took a counselor, reminding me, "She's still here. She's not leaving." It seems simple, but such a statement built a foundation to allow Jesus to root out some of Grandpa's pain.

Uneven ground may comprise refusing to budge from our current position. Maybe we assume we are 100% right, as we believe we occupy higher ground and our spouse is completely wrong. This posture leads to accusation and judgment rather than real forgiveness. Uneven terrain also means we start from a position from which we overlook the traits of our mate that facilitate forgiveness. Sadly, instead, we concentrate on the negative qualities that prevent forgiveness.

Consider John and Julie Gottman's research in *The Art and Science of Love*. They determined that couples who diminish negative perceptions and increase positive biases towards their spouses level the landscape in their relationship. Choosing to look at our spouses in the best possible light facilitates a level foundation.

The level soil at the base of the cross is where the redemptive story of marriage goes to find forgiveness. Our stories are brought together and placed smack-dab in the middle of His unending story. Forgiveness begins at the cross because the precious blood of Jesus purchased it and offers full forgiveness that can be extended to our mate.

Sincere love for one another and deep love for each other come from the redemptive sacrifice of a sinless Savior (i.e., 1 Peter 1:18-22). The ladder for forgiveness is mounted on the firmness of our decision to pursue the path to pardon.

UNFOLDING THE LADDER

We have a ladder in our storage shed that is a handy tool. It's portable, retractable, and collapsible. It folds down into a small package so that we can extend it to different levels. The engineering of the extension pieces is remarkable, as each piece  connects with and depends on the preceding segment. The expansions are unfolded piece by piece and stacked on each other to enable anyone climbing to reach greater heights. The invention is amazing and shows remarkable ingenuity in enabling places previously out of our reach to be accessed.

Once we place our lives on the ground level of forgiveness at the cross and find firm footing on the soil of grace, the Beatitudes describe what a blessed life looks like. The ladder of forgiveness helps all of us who want to forgive but still feel forgiveness is beyond our reach. We know we should forgive and admire those who do, but we're severely hurt. The wounds run deep. This is the position of so many marriages stuck in their wounds with no real path forward.

How do the beatitudes (Matthew 5:1-12) enable happiness, allow us to grow in mercy, and move on to real forgiveness? According to Jesus, the greatest happiness isn't found in places we normally look. They must be accessed by moving up to areas that were formerly out of our grasp. This explains why many people are trapped in unforgiveness and don't know how to start the journey to a new road that very few discover (Matthew 7:14). They start climbing in the wrong place.

Moving forward requires stepping down and starting at the bottom. The bottom begins with Jesus saying,

> Blessed are the poor in spirit,
> for theirs is the kingdom of heaven.
> MATTHEW 5:3 NIV

In his book, *Momentum: Pursuing God's Blessings Through the Beatitudes,* Colin Smith counters our reluctance to forgive. He further explains:

> It's when we find ourselves saying,
> "We don't have what it takes to forgive,"
> that God says to us,
> "I will dwell with you right here."
> Colin Smith

Empty hands are needed to receive what God wants to give us. We all need a divine boost of grace to access the first rung of the ladder. Self-effort and trying hard aren't the path forward in forgiveness. Surrender is. Couples need to dig deep into the well of grace to allow God to provide what they don't possess. Our inadequacy recognizes our inability to forgive without the grace God gives. Run to the cross. Stay at the cross. Live at the cross. There's life in His death.

The eight "Be's" in the Beatitudes unfold piece by piece, stacked one on top of another, and give us a road map for pursuing a blessed life. This blessed life leads to a happy marriage, while many pursue a happy marriage, thinking it leads to a joyful life. The Beatitudes are counterintuitive and allow us to stand in grace but strive for growth one rung at a time. Don't stay stuck at the bottom, lingering in the hurt and hate of unforgiveness.

Take the first step. Realize and recognize nobody has what it takes to make a marriage work. Then, and only then, are we ready for the first rung that leads to the next and eventually creates momentum in our marriages. Let's stretch our legs, flex our fingers to grasp the rails, and lift our foot as we start at rung one on the ladder of forgiveness.

RUNG ONE—GRIEVE THE OFFENSE

It's amusing that my wife installs the lights on top of our house for Christmas. I ask her to wait, but she'd rather get the party started. I mean, the 4th of July was last weekend (I kid. She waits until Labor Day!) I've offered to help because I know a guy who we can pay to do it.

One of my friends has a picture of me asking her what she is doing on a roof in 60 mph winds. He claims I said, "You're in serious trouble if you come down." I value my limbs too much to say something like that to Nancy.

Ladders can be dangerous. I know several people who have fallen off a ladder and done real harm to themselves. The first rung needs a safety check as the warning labels are read before we begin the ascent. Many people ignore the cautions on the ladder of forgiveness because they refuse to climb down off their high horse. Don't ignore the initial warnings when offended. Too often, our failure to read the room leads us to make interactions personal rather than setting the ladder on stable soil. After the fact, it is too late to acknowledge pitfalls and problems. Do it at the beginning.

Before ascending the first rung, we need to ensure a stable setup, so the ladder stays steady. A wobbly ladder prevents the ascent. It's also interesting that climbing a ladder is an individual affair, as a second person on a rung can cause the entire enterprise to crash. Forgiveness takes two, but it begins as a personal act and an individual decision to start the process. It isn't a quick fix or an easy practice, so we must ensure the frame is sturdy. An unsteady beginning can lead to a quick exit.

The work of forgiveness begins on the first rung, where we come eye-level with the hurt. We cannot move past the harm until we assess the depth of the damage. Rushing past the pain only leads to later and more profound hurt. Sweeping sorrow under the rug creates further problems down the road when the sadness surfaces and sabotages everything around us. Jesus said:

> Blessed are those who mourn,
> for they will be comforted.
> MATTHEW 5:4 NIV

We forfeit relief if we skip the grief. Grieving the offense gives credence to the state of our souls.

This reality reminds us that the incident must be serious or irritating enough to forgive. Some things in marriage must be overlooked as part of the personality of our mate or the way they are wired. Love allows little things to be overlooked and the relationship to move forward. Forgiveness needs to be reserved for acts that are big enough to lament. The process of pardon is also a recognition by the offender that a simple "sorry" to God or our mate and then continuing the same cycle is not the path of forgiveness. Instead, the offender grieves the harm, sees the cost, and makes a decisive break from the damage they inflicted. Authentic repentance leads to a change of direction.

Mourning is an integral part of forgiveness, where an admission is made that pain occurred and hurt happened. Forgiveness is initiated in the middle of the offense, not when emotions dissipate or time passes. Forgiveness isn't forgetting what happened, burying the issue, or minimizing the offense. The path to pardon doesn't excuse or condone unacceptable behavior.

Rung one on the forgiveness ladder acknowledges that an offense occurred, and it begins the process of climbing out of anger, hurt, and bitterness. The process of naming out loud exactly what occurred without speaking in generalities, as when you say, "I'm sorry for all the hurt I caused you." Real mourning involves specific, heartfelt sorrow for the damage done without deception or pretense. It runs to the cross in humility to find the help and hope needed to forgive.

RUNG TWO—GAIN PERSPECTIVE

The second rung gets you above the offense. The ascent is designed to move away from the incident and towards a new beginning. The climb helps us understand that forgiveness is not something that happens to us but is something done by us. Forgiveness is a path to pursue. The perspective we gain is the acknowledgment that we are both sinners in need of a Savior and a lot of grace. Jesus said:

> Blessed are the meek, for they will inherit the earth.
> MATTHEW 5:5 NIV

Meekness isn't mild or limp, but is unruliness brought under control. Think of a horse in a harness that allows its willfulness to be subdued and its strength directed to useful ends. Meekness is great strength under control. Colin Smith, in *Momentum: Pursuing God's Blessings Through the Beatitudes,* states, "It tames the temper, subdues the self, calms the passions, manages the impulses of the heart, and brings order out of the chaos of the soul." Meekness in marriage brings restraint as it harnesses our words to heal rather than to harm. Meekness refrains from opening fresh wounds to demand its pound of flesh because we were hurt.

Too often in marriage, we insult, demean, criticize, nag, complain, and explode without giving it a second thought. Meekness honors our spouse as a fellow heir to the kingdom, a human made in the image of God, and a deeply loved citizen of heaven despite their imperfections. Jesus didn't lash out on the cross, and He had much greater power than ours to unleash. Instead, lashed to the cross, Jesus offered words of grace and forgiveness. "Father, forgive them, for they do not know what they are doing," (Luke 23:34a [NIV, emphasis added]).

Meekness is restrained power. It gains perspective as it postures itself in a position of ratcheting down our abilities for the sake of harmony. Too often in marriage, we offer unsolicited advice in ways that demean our mate. Meekness relinquishes the right to say, "Step aside and let me show you how it's done." Husbands can choose to respond gently rather than harshly. Wives can offer encouragement rather than disparagement.

Gentleness attempts to communicate in ways our spouse can hear. Meekness sprouts forth from recognizing our inability to forgive and our need to grieve the harm we've caused. The bottom rung leads to the next level, not insisting on its own way and giving a proper estimate of our condition.

In fact, when we can't speak with grace, we ought to try silence, even in the face of aggression. Peter writes about this, saying:

> When they hurled their insults at him,
> he did not retaliate;
> when he suffered, he made no threats.
> Instead, he entrusted himself
> to him who judges justly.
> 1 PETER 2:23 NIV

Meekness is the model Jesus used to speak life rather than offer a defense. In marriage, the practice of meekness offers reconciliation instead of retaliation because the meek understand that those who need to be right will never be reconciled.

This rung is also the launching point of spiritual motivation. At this point on the forgiveness ladder, your energy shifts toward decisive action that will make a difference in your marriage. We want something different as we cultivate an appetite to do marriage in a distinct way. Jesus said:

> Blessed are those who hunger
> and thirst for righteousness,
> for they will be filled.
> MATTHEW 5:6 NIV

This value helps us recognize that we can acquire the tools to forgive with a simple request that Jesus says will be met. Don't hurry the process. Stay patient with God and yourself. Meekness is a learned skill.

RUNG THREE—DECIDE TO FORGIVE

The third rung on the ladder helps us see beyond the offense as we enter new and greater heights. Rung one is at eye level with the offense, and the second step gets you above the damage. As you ascend the ladder of forgiveness, the third rung allows for greater distance between the spouse and the offense. The larger gap enables us to see beyond the harm, de-escalate, and choose to forgive. Jesus reminds us:

> Blessed are the merciful,
> for they will be shown mercy.
> MATTHEW 5:7 NIV

Mercy is wider than forgiveness, but forgiveness goes longer and further than mercy. Mercy is clemency that, rather than return harm and repay evil for evil, decides to "overcome evil with good" (Romans 12:21b [NIV]). In a way, mercy is the perch on the ladder that is a steppingstone to exoneration. Pursue mercy, and you will reach forgiveness.

The generous stance of forgiveness gives an undeserved gift that arises from the character of God. He is described in a fourfold description on many occasions in the Old Testament as gracious, merciful, slow to anger, and abounding in love (Exodus 34:6). God's compassion displays this tender strength that acts on our behalf.

We can get even or stop the chain of evil and choose to forgive. Forgiveness releases our partner from liability and doesn't keep a record of the wrong to use as payback or revenge. The undertaking of forgiveness lets the offense go. It refuses to keep bringing the incident up in the future as a record of wrongs. We decide not to nurse the injury or repeatedly rehearse how wrong it was and how much it hurt. Instead, we take strides toward forgiving our spouse.

Rung three is where we say the words, "I forgive you." It may feel weird, but our feelings will eventually catch up to the deed. We plant both feet firmly on the rungs and cling to the forgiving grace of God. At the same time, we offer to our spouse what Jesus gave us—pardon freely given by His grace. It requires a single-mindedness of an undivided heart that follows hard after Jesus. No matter what, we will do what it takes to make it to the finish line.

Jesus states it like this:

> Blessed are the pure in heart,
> for they will see God.
> MATTHEW 5:8 NIV

We are proactive in pursuing purity, as it's not something behind us that was lost, but something ahead of us to be pursued and gained.

I set a goal of running a marathon before the age of 60. It was a BHAG goal (big, hairy, and audacious goal). I had never run further than a half-marathon and decided to double the distance and train as hard as possible to make sure I could make the distance. I was relentless in the pursuit of my desire to finish. I literally ran the soles off two pairs of shoes in preparation for the day with various preliminary runs. It was incredibly hard work, but I was unyielding in my hope of reaching the end of 26.2 miles. I was undivided in my commitment to complete the race and check the contest off my bucket list.

The day came in November 2020, and alterations were made to the marathon because of Covid precautions. Things I took for granted during my preparation were taken off the table. We literally ran out of water in the marathon from mile sixteen to mile twenty-one. I experienced dehydration and excruciating muscle cramps, but one thing kept me locked in. I didn't come to Cocoa Beach, Florida, to start a race. I came to finish. I was determined not to quit. The recurring thought that set my pace and captured my heart was simple: run the race to the tape. Don't stop. Don't give up. Don't give in. The reward is down the road.

There's a medal and photo evidence in my office to commemorate the accomplishment of my goal. I ran two marathons that day: my first and my last. I threw my shoes into the ocean to make sure I wouldn't be tempted to try that task ever again. The most worthwhile part of my day was seeing my wife, Nancy, standing in the middle of the road, urging me on. I broke the tape because I saw the finish line. I completed the course with tears in my eyes, a lump in my throat, and severe cramps in my legs. It took a while in the first-aid tent to get rehydrated and back on my feet. I drank gallons of Gatorade and refueled with protein bars and several bananas.

A single-minded pursuit of purity allows us to fix our eyes on Jesus. With perseverance, we run our race marked out in advance (Hebrews 12:1-2). Will we throw off everything hindering us from finishing the marital race God has marked out for us? Do we recognize that persevering in our marriage and throwing off entangling sin is a testimony to those around us? Can we see the finish line? Do we hear the heavenly applause of our Savior, imploring us not to quit? Listen to the cadence on the track: "Don't stop running." We didn't come to start a race. We came to finish.

Forgiveness allows us to complete what we started. Forgiveness allows us to see the finish line. Forgiveness envisions our spouses at the tape, urging us to run to the end. We may fall and get back up. We may lose breath and double over in pain. We may struggle and need to rejoin the race after a quick break. Here's the bottom line: Forgiveness paves the way to seeing a greater reward. We can break the tape if we see the finish line and decide to forgive.

RUNG FOUR—REPEAT UNTIL IT TAKES

The last rung is a reiteration of what we've already done as we commit to forgiving the offense. The greater distance from the offense doesn't mean we aren't tempted to climb back down the ladder and rehearse the hurt. In fact, it's harder to stay at the top and complete the task than it is to go down the rungs to the bottom and pick the hurt back up.

We should only descend the ladder to come down from our high horse position—that forgiveness isn't possible. We will almost certainly be convinced we never really forgave in the first place. Thoughts may assail you with a conviction that forgiveness never happened. But as someone once said, "The flock of birds may fly over your head, but you can stop them from building a nest in your hair."

This is the action of a peacemaker, not the avoidance of one keeping the peace. It initiates the words of Jesus that say:

> Blessed are the peacemakers,
> for they will be called children of God.
> **MATTHEW 5:9 NIV**

This final beatitude is the result of the previous pursuits.

The order and progress up the ladder of forgiveness as we ascend to the top require increased concentration and stretching further to reach our destination. It's why peacemakers are hard to find in marriage and life. Satan does everything he can to stir up strife and then warms himself at the fire of the fight.

Whatever state our marriage is in requires us to make things better by peacemaking to the best of our ability. When peace is lost, we go out of our way to restore it. When peace is disrupted, we use whatever influence we are given to contribute to the peace of our families. When a marriage is humming on all cylinders, our task is not to let down but to double down and keep it that way. This leads to shalom, which is more than the absence of conflict; it includes enjoying all that is good. Marriages flourish when spouses strive for peace. We do everything we can to secure personal peace inside us and offer relational peace around us.

This is the ladder of forgiveness that identifies us as children of God. Forgiveness allows us to reflect the likeness of our Heavenly Father. Like Jesus, we surrender our rights in order to take steps toward reconciliation. We don't avoid trouble and back off; we move toward our mate in courage, as marriage isn't for the faint of heart. In some ways, marriage is the most dangerous job in the world. Jesus modeled what we should emulate as He laid down His life before a scintilla of love was reciprocated. That is our call as we love our spouse. Love goes first.

Recognize the issues. Deal with them early. Practice restraint, especially with your tongue. Prepare for a long journey and do everything in your power to take steps toward forgiveness and making peace. Forgiveness is hard work. Peacemaking is an intense effort. Marriage is intentionally scaling the ladder of forgiveness repeatedly. The work doesn't end until the day Jesus calls you to Himself. This is the tough work of forgiveness, but the relationship still must be repaired.

Remedy means working together to make repairs. Steps to reconciliation are the next topic as we learn how to have hard conversations. It's enough for now to relish this: Jesus didn't climb down from the cross and rehearse the hurts he received. Instead, Jesus lashed himself with love to the cross so we might be forgiven.

Love led Him there, and love kept Him there as He reconciled us to God. Jesus took our enmity and refused to let sin slide. By His grace, Jesus took a stand so we could stand on and in His righteousness.

That's amazing grace! That's amazing love! His first step was a holy movement toward us in love. His ultimate sacrifice paved the path to eternity. Only one ladder climbs to heaven—Jesus is the only way.

Chapter 8

Hard Talks and Carry-Ons

Most men cower in the corner at a simple request: "Can we talk?" I know my repeated thought is, *What have I done now?* I fire up my mental directory and begin to pull out files that might somehow relate to the discussion that is about to ensue. Often, my calculation isn't even in the ballpark. I quickly deduce she's probably about to address the pile of dishes stacked in the sink. I smartly pivot by requesting that we just go out to eat with our friends, knowing that avoiding the plates will prevent upending her equilibrium concerning undone tasks.

What I didn't know was that we were about to begin what is informally known as a "hard talk" or, in marital shorthand, a brawl. Nancy had had a day: She was in deep water, up to her neck, and in a pickle, to string a bunch of idioms together. My casual mention of supper with another couple (that's dinner for you non-Southerners, bless your hearts) led to a quick-fire exchange. She said she had already undressed, put on her jammies, and made spaghetti.

Now, I'm a man and clueless, so I replied as expected, "So, put on your clothes, store the noodles in the Tupperware, and we'll leave in a jiffy. No problem."

Uhm. Wrong. Big Problem! The grenade was about to be dropped; the pin was already pulled, and verbal shrapnel was about to scatter. Now, with my request, I'm up to my neck in deep water. You get the picture.

What I didn't understand was what putting on her jammies meant to her. The act of getting casual entails saying *sayonara* to any outside commitments in the world beyond our front door. In layman's terms, the day is DONE. OVER. When the everyday wardrobe is removed, the undies hung up, and the pajamas put on, there are no negotiations for a different verdict. And, if I pushed it, I'd be wearing the spaghetti.

Here's the scoop: I love Nancy more than I can express. I love how her brown eyes gleam and how her forehead crinkles. I love it when she sings and how she sits in rapt attention when talking to anyone. I love every inch of her body, every contour of her face, and every trait of her personality, but I understand little of anything about how she thinks.

I often wish I could do a mind meld, but I'm certain that would melt every neural circuit I have. These comprehension gaps between us create difficult discussions that can happen anytime, anywhere, and anyplace, including while wearing pajamas. So, I've planned a trip for you and your spouse that will fly through some turbulence we've already encountered.

The flight might save you some steps because we've already done the turnaround caused by destructive patterns of communication. We've navigated the runway of feeling unheard by one another and dealt with being stuck on conversational tarmacs with no end in sight. We've come out on the other side with a stronger marriage and better handles on how to love each other. So, grab a suitcase, get your boarding pass, buckle up, and join me on a trip to a distant destination: the island of hard conversations.

BEFORE YOU BOARD, SET UP YOUR TALK

"I've been everywhere, man. Of travel, I've had my share, man." Those lines are the lyrics of the Johnny Cash tune, "I've Been Everywhere," and the list of destinations Cash croons about whets the appetite of my wanderlust. It makes me want to go to Fond du Lac, which is about as accessible as the South Pole.

Nancy and I really haven't been everywhere, but we have marked 49 states off our bucket list and hope to visit the final one soon. Wanderlust doesn't happen without groundwork. Preparation is the key to wayfaring with fewer snags. It means snagging boarding passes, making reservations, grabbing confirmations, mapping destinations, and downloading mobile apps. It's not the fun part of travel, but the homework makes the trip work.

The legwork for conflict is about as much fun as airport screening with the TSA. We've decided that hospital gowns and flip-flops are the best garments for screening, and we always weigh our luggage with a hand scale to ensure we don't get penalized for our load. I've always wondered why the security screeners don't look fabulous, considering how many health and beauty products they confiscate. One thing is for sure: With TSA agents, you need to plan for the uncomfortable. Prepare for intrusive pat-downs, looking through your undergarments, terse announcements, and other invasions without invitation.

Preparing in advance for TSA agents to snoop through everything and ask about anything reminds couples that planning for hard talks will allow intrusive interactions to begin. The preliminary homework is designed so we might check ourselves before we wreck ourselves. Groundwork doesn't mean unplanned trips (conflict) won't pop up. But it does diminish the amount and intensity of these impromptu exchanges. We must prepare the setting so that it's not so upsetting to deal with the issues on the table. Winging discussions may seem easier, but painless seldom ends in better. The Bible calls this practice "prudence" or, to use King James' version verbiage, "walking circumspectly."

> See then that you walk circumspectly,
> not as fools but as wise,
> redeeming the time,
> because the days are evil.
> **EPHESIANS 5:15-16 NKJV**

We are called to look around carefully to ensure the undertaking is done wisely as we set up our talk. *The prudent setup acts as love handles in conflict that we can use to handle our underlying baggage.*

CHECK YOUR CARRY-ON LUGGAGE

The beginning of a hard talk needs to deal with the main currents beneath an issue. Douglas Stone says in *Difficult Conversations* that there are three carry-on components or underlying structures to what's happening within every discussion. We need to examine the clues that will cue us into some of the intentions and assumptions that prevent learning and listening in conversations.

There's often a significant gap when we are talking between what we are saying and what we are thinking. Monitoring the distortions and disruptions that assault our thoughts and emotions can help us prevent predictable errors. We can gather clues with some C.U.Es. that help us identify the three ongoing dialogues as we interact:

1. **C**onverse about what has happened or what should happen. This step includes exploring different perceptions in the story, sharing the impact on each other, and discovering how we each contributed to the misunderstanding. This is "What's the story here?"
2. **U**nderlying feelings are pinpointed within ourselves that color the dialogue as we decide what emotions are unhelpful or inappropriate. Attempt to validate our partner's feelings and avoid judging what is being shared. This is "What should we do with our emotions?"
3. **E**go and identity are determined to enable us to deal with how conflict may threaten us psychologically, use coping skills to maintain mental equilibrium, and discern what each person is saying to themselves about themselves. This is "What does this conversation say about me?"

We all carry things in our souls that need sifting through. Rather than fighting about who is right, we are attempting to be better at conflict so we can battle for intimacy. It's conflict instead of combat; combat crushes our spirits, while conflict can buttress our souls. Scrutinizing our carry-on conversations, stowaway emotions, and hidden identity issues will enable us to stay connected without losing our uniqueness.

One psychologist suggests that the difficulty with couples is that we often interpret hurtful behavior with negative automatic viewpoints that are well-rehearsed from past encounters. A path forward is to "take captive every thought to make it obedient to Christ" (2 Corinthians 10:5b [NIV]). Filtering thoughts allows us to establish a new frame of reference. This, in turn, allows us to take responsibility for what considerations we bring into the disagreement. Clearing our carry-on baggage will lighten our load.

Frequent travelers recognize that airlines weigh luggage before boarding is allowed. Similarly, we must deal with the baggage we lug around as couples. The emotional and relational baggage each spouse carries can be loaded into hard talks. But couples pay a steep price for refusing to unpack and unload the dysfunction from their past. The author of Hebrews implores us:

> Let us lay aside every weight,
> and the sin which so easily besets us,
> and let us run with perseverance
> the race that is set before us.
> HEBREWS 12:1 KJV

We need to do the arduous task of culling out of our communication patterns what is unnecessary to the topic at hand. Sometimes, this means talking to a trusted friend, mentor, pastor, or counselor to help dispose of unexamined personal beliefs. A marriage is only as healthy as the two people living inside it. Lightening the load can lift the relationship to a higher place.

HEAD TO THE GATE

I don't know about you, but for me, the trip from baggage check to the gate is usually a harried mental and physical exercise to gather my thoughts and my belongings. I run through my checklist to ensure that I'm ready to go through the screening process:

- Rifling through my belongings for my passport,

- Making sure my pockets are empty,
- Checking for my phone and boarding pass,
- Wondering if I locked my car, and
- Making sure my pants stay up if I have to remove my belt.

Often, I need to take a deep breath or a quick seat and calm the six million considerations racing through my mind.

Isn't this true as we go through prepping for a hard talk? It's not only what needs to be said, but also how it will be said. Stepping back and examining what's necessary to communicate and what isn't essential helps filter through the fluff and assists in landing on real priorities.

Did it matter that much that my spouse decided to stay home in her jammies rather than go out? There's always another opportunity to gather with friends, and our relationship is too valuable to constantly live defensively. Often, when we take time to gather our thoughts, we remember that the reactions of our spouse aren't personal. Instead, the response can be caused by the circumstances of life swirling around, like personal exhaustion or a pending deadline at work.

Many times, hard conversations are derailed by jumping at hyper-speed to hyperbole. When we craft our complaint as an accusation, it's almost a given that it will fail from the get-go. We must eliminate blanket statements that will lead to dead ends, such as:

- "You never . . . "
- "You always . . ."
- "You continually . . . "
- "You started . . . "
- "Would you be reasonable?"

Dialing down the "you" statements and even opting to employ "I feel like . . . " phrases foster an assurance that we aren't imposing our views or accusing our spouses. The goal isn't to provoke our mate but to connect with our partner. Thinking about what you are saying is important, but examining how you will say it is also vital.

EXAMINE YOUR BOARDING PASS

I do almost all the homework as we prepare for trips, including booking the flight, entering the pertinent information, and checking in for the takeoff. I convert points to miles, search the quickest connections, and scour the internet for killer deals. We signed up for an expedited screening program called TSA Precheck that allows us to skip some of the time and hassle at airport security. We can leave liquids in our overnight kits, keep our shoes and belts on, and save time in the security line. We got TSA Precheck for free because of credit card perks. I also completed the application for a known traveler number on our documentation.

What I sometimes fail to do is EXAMINE THE BOARDING PASS. The boarding pass is important because it designates where we are going and how we will get there. Too many crucial conversations are derailed because we fail to stay focused on the situation and the destination. Then we end up crash-landing on runways we never intended to visit.

I now know from hindsight that they won't let anyone through screening without the designation of TSA special status, no matter how vehemently the point is conveyed. Without the stamp of a known traveler number, the individual in question goes to another queue—or the pile of peasants in the ordinary screening line.

Nancy's pre-TSA clearance did not appear on her boarding pass. I did what came automatically and proceeded through pre-check. In hindsight, I thoughtlessly moved forward as Nancy not-so-silently switched lines. I booked the ticket, and she got the shaft. I waited at Chick-fil-A while she got filleted. It wasn't my finest moment. She felt irritated. I felt unappreciated, and the end could have been expected.

The lesson to learn is that you are responsible for checking your own boarding pass (I kid. I kid . . . Sort of). Conflict is complicated because it contains a host of interacting and interlocking issues and intentions that are impossible to assess accurately. The likelihood is significant that you have contributed to the problem because we all maintain biases and exhibit behaviors that add to the chaos. A flight's boarding pass permits a passenger to enter restricted areas at airports and eventually get on the flight. Marriage allows our spouse to go into places no other human can access. Vulnerability, accessibility, and flexibility are essential for making a marriage hum.

How can each spouse take responsibility to make sure they are ready to engage in a hard conversation? How can we examine our individual expectations to better get to the heart of the issue? The process is not exhilarating; in fact, it is as pedestrian and flat-out mundane as it comes. But it paves the way for a better discussion. There are a few items to examine on our marital boarding passes before we can begin to talk effectively.

EXAMINE YOUR SECRET CONTRACTS

The assumption in our marriage is that I would handle the travel plans. We didn't sign an agreement or even shake hands. Kim and Penn Holderness say assigning roles and responsibilities is one of the autopilot pieces we do daily through default and routine. This way, we don't have to negotiate every single aspect of our lives.

Nancy does laundry, beds, most cooking, and household activities. I grocery shop, pay bills, write books and sermons, and take out the trash. That's not the full list, but you get the gist of the idea. The book *Everybody Fights* uses the phrase "secret contracts" as the silent agreements couples make to allow each spouse to trek habitual grooves. This works if both partners are in sync and don't want an adjustment.

Grooves can lead to graves if we refuse to alter responsibilities and roles when life changes. Resentment can build if we keep doing what we've always done without examining why and how it is done. These assignments can be more than roles because sometimes they are about who our partner expects us to be.

We all occupy places and spaces that initially feel natural and normal in our marriage. Still, we may morph into routine instead of authentic desires. This is where secret contracts need to be negotiated at the right time, in the right way, and with the right tone and attitude. This is part of the boarding pass for any hard conversation and part of the preliminaries that facilitate smoother landings.

EXAMINE YOUR APPRECIATION

These silent assignments expose another issue that impacts our marital harmony: expressing appreciation. Lack of voiced gratitude increases frustration if we don't say *thank you* in observable ways. Nancy and I's battle over the boarding pass was complicated because I didn't feel appreciated. We assume our spouse knows we are grateful, but the truth is a verbal say-so is a huge pick-me-up.

Most of us assume our spouses know we welcome their contributions. But we cut corners on common courtesy to our own detriment. A lack of declared delight for our spouses' tasks creates relational angst. We too often verbalize criticisms the instant something happens. We withhold praise and dole it out in small doses. Curt corrections create strife, while public displays of appreciation (PDA) often increase the chance that good behaviors will be repeated.

When we aren't dialed in consistently as a spouse, and our partner is relegated to the bottom of our to-do list, we fail to lubricate with love and appreciate with praise. Paul states it well:

> Do not let any unwholesome talk
> come out of your mouths,
> but only what is helpful for building others up
> according to their needs,
> that it may benefit those who listen.
> EPHESIANS 4:29 NIV

I've watched people in their 60s put handwritten notes of encouragement and praise on their refrigerators. I keep notes from decades ago of people who took the time to say, "*Job well done.*" My desk drawer is stuffed with notes from my wife that immediately lift my mood when I read them. Prompt, specific thank yous that treat our spouses better than strangers are a clear path to making hard conversations a little less daunting. Appreciation that is shared consistently will lessen the amount and intensity of difficult discussions in the future.

EXAMINE EMOTIONAL BORDERS

Examining emotional borders is another piece of our marital boarding passes that seems matter-of-fact. We innately believe that our partners view the broader world in the same way that we do.

When we share a point of view with someone, we feel connected and close and think life is hunky-dory. Consequently, when our spouses respond to a situation with a completely distinct reaction, it can lead to an emotional funk. I tend to be low-key, in control, and not particularly sentimental in dealing with many situations.

Nancy loves this part of me until she doesn't. She is wired differently. She is in tune, in the moment, vividly expressive, and extremely sentimental. I love this part of her until I don't. Difficulty comes when we think we must recalibrate our reactions to match the other person's feelings. Such recalibrations lead to inauthenticity and telling each other half-truths, which Scripture reminds you to avoid.

> Therefore each of you must put off falsehood
> and speak truthfully to your neighbor,
> for we are members of one body.
> EPHESIANS 4:25 NIV

Mister Rogers reminds you that the neighbor, called your "spouse," is to be valued and appreciated as uniquely crafted by your Creator. Your mate is not a clone that completes you, but an original composition that complements you. Together, one-flesh intimacy is designed to bring out the whole you and allow you to be who you really are.

Don't sacrifice your authentic self to create a pseudo-connection that will disappear beneath tsunamis of emotional waves. *Be you. Be real. Be different. Be the best version of yourself that you can possibly be.*

- It's not your responsibility to make things better. It is your responsibility to do your best.

- It's not your job to solve your spouse's problems. It's not your spouse's job to solve your problems.
- Hard conversations don't define who I am.
- You don't have to agree with feelings to validate what is being shared. Your mate will feel better knowing it's not all in their head.
- Love your husband or wife through the emotional funk.

GETTING THROUGH SECURITY

The final piece of setting up your talk is security clearance. Airport personnel check your passport, screen your carry-ons, and lead you through a metal detector to clear you to sit at your gate. Getting to the gate means you are all clear to board the aircraft. This is the next step in the process of preparation for hard conversations. The screener may ask several questions as you walk through the line. "Did you pack your own bags?" "Has anyone unknown to you asked you to carry anything on board?" "Has the bag been out of your possession?" The assessment is designed to reveal if it's you who is showing up and what you are carrying with you.

As you prepare for a difficult dialogue, you need to get settled. Recognize that two distinctly different people are about to prod one another, x-ray the bones of the issues, and examine each response. Such a screening process makes it crucial for you to pack your conversational bags and bring your emotional possessions to the meeting. You must communicate assertively, take responsibility for your feelings and actions, and decline to concentrate on your spouse as the problem.

Don't carry something into a difficult conversation from a previous fight to reopen for discussion. This will only lengthen the conflict and make the process much more difficult. Save other issues for another leg of the trip. Show up as yourself and don't make your partner guess what's in your bag of complaints. Open the conversation with what's on your mind.

Deal with the issue at hand and recognize that each person brings a particular style of resolving conflict into the screening process. Some people are highly expressive in communicating, while others are reflective before they offer a viewpoint. Many spouses avoid speaking the truth, seeking to gloss over troubles to maintain their mate's approval. Other spouses decisively state their views with no thought about accommodating their partner's feelings.

The way you are wired in your temperament is non-negotiable. However, a marital duo says each partner can stress or moderate traits to accommodate their spouse. Realize that the style of interaction you bring into a conversation is adjustable in the moment. Grace is available to help facilitate a healthier step towards connection.

Travel brings us closer together, even as it reveals how different our personalities are. We went to Graceland in Memphis, Tennessee, to pay homage to Elvis Presley's surprisingly humble digs. We saw bad landscape paintings, pink and mauve tiled bathrooms, and an old chest of drawers.

I'm convinced Elvis would have moved out of his personal Heartbreak Hotel long ago. It's still stuck in the 70s with dark blue carpet, red leather chairs, and Tiffany lighting. Graceland contains a ton of Elvis paraphernalia, jumpsuits, markers of accomplishments, and even the plot where Elvis is buried. Nancy lingered at every exhibit, read every script, examined each carpet stain, and reminisced about her childhood. I didn't. I had one goal to accomplish: Get to the exit sign and pull Nancy off Elvis's grave.

My main approach in life is to race through, rarely taking time to stop and smell the roses. I have goals to achieve, tasks to accomplish, and boxes to check. Nancy, on the other hand, lives deeply in the moment. She enjoys immensely what we already have: a community we love, a church that is making a tremendous impact, and a home that is a nesting spot. She could sit on our patio and relish our backyard for days. I'd get bored in a hurry. This is also how we fight. I'm in a hurry to get to what's *next*, while she wants to put off *next* to deal with *now*. Do you see how this might lead to interesting relational dynamics?

We've learned methods you can employ while interacting with your spouse that mimic the activity of a careful screening agent. Make eye contact. Let your spouse know you are attempting to say, "I am with you; I am here; I am tuned in." The goal of any security check, whether in marriage or at the airport, is to make us feel safe rather than invaded and neglected. Too often, we use evasive maneuvers that prevent closeness rather than enable it. Security should create an attachment that enables our partner to be close, available, observant, and caring. Detachment happens when we don't feel connected, are emotionally adrift, and distance ourselves from our mates.

How often do we hear our spouses choke out a forced "I'm sorry" that really says, "Please don't be angry?" Often, "I'm sorry" is used to stop the fracas. Employing apologies as a magic wand to fix whatever is amiss doesn't bring us closer or strengthen our attachment. Using this tactic does not ease our spouse's pain; it's an attempt to alleviate our own discomfort.

False apologies don't address the issue or ease hurt feelings in the process of clearing security. The good news is that there is a way to make the interaction draw our partner closer to us. It's a method Jesus frequently used in His encounters throughout the Bible: the art of the question.

Ask for more information by using clarifying questions. Follow-up questions help you follow through. Don't make assumptions; ask for more information. We tell ourselves stories about what we've seen and heard. Many times, the stories are clouded as partners create victims ("It's not my fault"), villains ("It's your fault"), and the powerless ("There's nothing else I can do").

Kim and Penn Holderness use a concept called the Simple Switch as an antidote to avoidance and protest responses, which often create distance. It's as simple as the common phrase my Life Group teacher uses when someone responds to a question: "Tell me more." These three little words are simple and affirming, and can defuse tension and keep conflict from becoming combat.

Here's a sample of similar responses that are clarifying questions that ask for more information rather than lead to protest or shutdown:

- "You've mentioned this before. Do you mind explaining why this matters so much to you right now?"
- "I'd like to know where you are coming from. Can you help me understand?"
- "I'm not sure I'm following. How did you arrive at this point?"
- "That's an interesting thought. Tell me more."
- "I'm not quite grasping what you are asking me. Can you ask it again differently?"

These questions are a better approach than a terse "Fine," a dismissive eye roll, or a flippant response that quickly reveals irritation instead of anticipation. This is very much a long-term project and will take practice. Nancy will always linger, looking at the shag carpet while I rush off to jump on the tour bus, and the struggle will continue.

However, we have found that we are more connected if we take a minute and attempt to hear what our spouse is saying. And we don't have to resort to temper tantrums to get the other person's attention. Maybe next time, I'll linger with her during a tour of Heartbreak Hotel. I'll attempt not to step on her "Blue Suede Shoes" and keep her from being "Lonesome Tonight."

I am, you know [*wait for it*], just a hunk, a hunk of burning love. I'll see myself out with this: "Thank you, thank you very much."

Chapter 9

Aisle Seats and Runways

The only place to plant your behind on an aircraft is in the aisle seat. The masses have watched *The Wedding Singer*'s Drew Barrymore (Julia Sullivan) pine for Adam Sandler (Robbie Hart). She wants to spend the rest of her life with a husband who will allow her to occupy a window seat. I mean, who doesn't want to sing "Grow Old with You" on their 50th wedding anniversary? (If you haven't caught this classic movie, queue it up immediately—I'll wait for you.) Despite the movie nostalgia, window seats are the worst (if you don't count the middle seat, which is like raisins in a trail mix).

Think about it. From the window seat, you must scooch over two people, using compromising positions to access the walkway with vain hopes that the other passengers will move over an inch to accommodate you. The aisle seat breathes *Braveheart* freedom as you aren't squeezed against a window and cemented into a cubbyhole while your middle seat companion leans their head against your shoulder. Plus, the aisle seat accommodates weak bladders and gives you an armrest that's only yours.

Who thinks this view is completely bonkers? My beautiful bride, Nancy, prefers placing her nose in the window to take in the scenery. It helps that she's petite and flexible, and I'm *neither* diminutive *nor* able to bend my body in any uncomfortable positions. She claims she doesn't enjoy getting clipped by the snack trolleys and rarely gets up during the flight, anyway. Does it surprise any of you one iota that we take opposite points of view or seats?

PREPARING FOR TAKEOFF

The reality is that opposites attract, and as the old cliché says, "Opposites often attack." Nancy and I don't fight nearly as often as we used to, but we held our own in earlier days. Experts say it takes 10,000 hours to become skillful in anything, so we are way past the time needed to qualify as proficient in the art of pugnacious confrontations.

One thing that helped us do crucial conversations more artfully is reviewing where things went wrong when we've had a big blowup. If you've ever watched the brothers, Peyton and Eli Manning, break down a *Monday Night Football* contest, you get the gist of this exercise. They give laid-back analysis from their vast experience, analyzing the game as it happens. It's a wide-angle look by two wily veteran quarterbacks, examining what's happening in the huddle and on the field.

Couples (like Nancy and me) can employ a strategy comparable to the insight given by veteran quarterbacks as the game unfolds. The difference is that Nancy and I replay how we fought (after the fight). This allows us to improve discourse in our marriage, enables better interaction during crucial conversations down the road, and become more productive and intentional in the long run. Replays and repair attempts prepare us for smoother take-offs and easier landings on the conversational runway.

FIND YOUR SEAT

Another phase in preparing for takeoff is scanning the aisles, securing your carry-on luggage, and finding your seating assignment. Often, there are mix-ups or confusion about the place your posterior is supposed to occupy. Frequently, you pray for an upgrade to an exit row with more legroom to make the flight more enjoyable. The uber-blessed gets bumped to the elite seats of first class, which is a whole different zip code behind the holy of holies (at least that's what I've heard). Undoubtedly, I'd break out in the *Hallelujah Chorus* if I snagged a reclining luxury pod in first class and secured all the extra perks.

In real estate and relationships, the key is location, location, location. Have you ever witnessed someone on an airplane take a call on speaker in the middle of a flight? Uh, no! No one wants to hear about Aunt Mildred and her hemorrhoids, ice packs, and compresses. The places couples choose to start tough talks are one component of getting the conversation off the ground (see what I did there?). Do you pay attention to where your dialogues occur? You can doom an exchange from the beginning with a poor choice of sites.

According to the accounts of the life of Jesus, our Savior withdrew to three different environments to retreat and recharge: near water (Mark 3:7), on a mountain (Mark 6:46), and in the desert (Luke 5:16). We pastored in Tucson and had all three available, but we now live in a location where none are accessible. Likewise, many of our difficult discussions occur in less-than-perfect locales, and interruptions such as Amazon deliveries, Alexa notifications, and wailing children often invade our spaces.

To clarify, couples must figure out a time when children are occupied, choose the best possible environment, close their doors, and silence their notifications. Unsuitable settings involve places such as Ikea (Swedish for irate spouse), while neutering a pet, during a tax audit, while being pulled over by a Highway Patrol, or in front of six girls in your living room during a sleepover. Part of the framework of good discussions includes designating areas that are off-limits and citing some realms where engagement is possible. Proverbs 27:14 says:

> If anyone loudly blesses their neighbor
> early in the morning, it will be taken as a curse.
> PROVERBS 27:14 NIV

A good deed done at the wrong time can lead to bad outcomes.

> [There's] a time to embrace
> and a time to refrain from embracing.
> ECCLESIASTES 3:5b NIV [Emphasis added]

There are no perfect times, but agreeing on a negotiated timeframe is time well spent. Inappropriate moments that should be avoided include a hunting trip with loaded weapons, riding tandem on a Harley-Davidson, soaring in a hot-air balloon, or during judo lessons. The odds are that someone will get severely hurt.

Sometimes, we sabotage a session from the start by beginning at inopportune moments when there is insufficient leeway to complete the conversation. It's like opening a wound to drain, closing it off, allowing it to fester for hours, and reopening the injury later. We need to reserve optimum periods to prioritize discussions because poorly chosen moments take longer to resolve, create more tension, and leave us unfocused and unmotivated to deal with the issues on the table. Sidelining the topic with a stark, "I don't want to talk about this now," doesn't help unless an alternative is offered. Some moments need to be labeled out of bounds because, when we are less than at our best, we prolong the pain. Instead, we need to choose optimum periods so we can use every ounce of energy to create meaningful momentum. Every couple needs to incorporate peak periods, allowing back-and-forth dialogue to avoid a rough landing.

STAY IN YOUR SEAT

I expect that many of you think it's time to land the plane in the run-up to a hard talk. But these preliminary steps aren't accomplished in a single setting. In fact, the setup for better outcomes is a lifetime process. Initial strides remind us that what's in our heads doesn't have to be said, and we can talk to ourselves as we talk to one another. This will allow us to settle into the interaction and sit in the moment.

Nothing seems worse on a flight than a seatmate who refuses to stay buckled in. Passengers who constantly get up and rummage through the overhead bin, lean into our space, rifle through the personal carry-ons under their seats, and repeatedly visit the lavatory get on our last nerve. It's aggravating, leading us to take umbrage and creating the possibility of escalation. Most passengers would prefer to switch to another cabin rather than deal with a rude companion on a flight. The urge is strong in such a setting to unload on the irritating person and let them have a piece of our mind.

Marriages are similar when spouses refuse to stay in their seats during discussions. This maneuver is a conversational dodge that attempts to avoid the topic at hand. Pivoting away from the issue we're debating and addressing other concerns creates an overwhelming sense that we've moved away from the specific problem. Pivots often enter personal and emotional territories where meaning becomes precarious. The result is that we raise the overall temperature of the dialogue. We attack our spouse's position and end up bouncing around all over the place to escape the problem in the queue. Rather than finding a way through the difficulty, we attempt to find a way around or out and end up making a mess that is harder to clean up. It doesn't mean the other matters that emerge during a fight don't matter, but those things can be filed away to return to in future interactions.

Boarding airplanes and participating in meaningful discussions are attempts at intentionality instead of wandering off script. Reexamining where things went wrong clarifies the emotions that flooded our minds while we were overwhelmed and swallowed up by our feelings. This habit allows course corrections as we find our way to more productive interactions.

In a sense, staying in the moment instead of leaving our seat, searching for a parachute, and pulling the ripcord is an affirmation that we are on this journey together. Too many partners attempt to leave the scene and avoid an argument by jumping out of harm's way. It's ludicrous to assume we can jump out of a commercial aircraft.

Likewise, it's an exercise in futility to avoid conflict. Couples must find their seat and stay seated during difficult conversations to ensure the discussion doesn't leave the runway and end up in the ditch.

BUCKLE YOUR SEATBELT

The act of buckling our seatbelt reminds us that misunderstanding is a natural part of marriage. Conflict happens. No matter how intensely a husband and wife love one another, they will eventually need to buckle up and buckle down because conflict in marriage is unavoidable. Knowing how to fight constructively instead of destructively is critical to couples living in harmony and maintaining intimacy. It's one thing to fall in love and quite another to stay in love. Research shows that how well couples handle disagreements determines the long-term happiness of a marriage. Most skirmishes erupt over relatively minor issues and often occur more intensely and more frequently about the same subjects. It's why we need to buckle up; the ride can be bumpy.

Most conflicts reflect the differences in our values and our personalities. It includes underlying issues that are the heart of what is causing our consternation. Often, a power play ensues to ensure our personalities shine and our values emerge.

Frequently, one spouse will play the part of the martyr and reason, "I'm above it all." Or "I'm not about to dignify that with a response" as a means of setting the agenda in advance. According to one marital duo, refusing to engage with your partner, or stonewalling, is a means of asserting control and seizing power. Sometimes, there's a need to make a fuss, get up in their business, and bring it up. The odds of the hard talk blowing over or going away are like winning the lottery. It. Won't. Happen. We need to learn to fight and do it right.

The emerging issues are often rooted in how we would prefer to experience life. I'd rather live in the moment and say yes to experiences, while Nancy wants to save money for a rainy day in a 401(k). Most marital inventories explore checkups on issues and lead to difficult dialogues. Finances are often at the top of the list.

Working through money issues can create enormous angst as discussions quickly get personal. Conversations escalate from school zone speed limits to autobahn pace, and comparisons ensue about who spent how much on what. We take money talks personally, and exchanges about financial matters will be among the most difficult issues we face as a couple.

PUTTING ON THE OXYGEN MASK

Buckling down in preparation to discuss problematic areas like finances, parenting, sex, and roles enables us to choose our battles carefully. Picking battles cautiously will allow each other to see the subject clearly. Marital battles become persistent when the source of the frustration isn't the point of the conversation.

This is where the flight attendant's instructions are useful, as they explain before take-off the "where's," "what's," and "what-ifs." "Should an emergency occur, you need to put your oxygen mask on first, before attempting to help those around you." This seems self-serving and backward, but upon reflection, it makes absolute sense.

If I'm sucking air personally, I can't contribute to the relationship in a healthy fashion. There are ways to stay in the moment and deal with the flood of negative emotions that emerge during a crucial conversation. Even when we take steps to navigate difficult discussions fruitfully, adverse thoughts occur with regularity in the middle of an exchange that generates hurt and contains the possibility of hijacking the whole interaction.

When we are overwhelmed, our physiology responds with our fight, flight, or freeze reactions. Our heart speeds up, adrenaline kicks in, blood pressure elevates, pupils dilate, and hormones activate. In these moments, if we immediately react, we'll either attack vehemently, be defensive verbally, withdraw suddenly, or shut down entirely.

It's here that we need to remember to breathe our own oxygen. As we pause, going to God in prayer helps us avoid pushing buttons, fighting dirty, and using the four horsemen of apocalyptic fighting styles (criticism-violence, contempt-defiance, defensiveness-avoidance, and stonewalling-silence). Anytime the dialogue goes in the wrong direction, we can backtrack in our mind, attempt to understand our own feelings, and endeavor to ease the angst in ourselves and with our mates. Negative experiences are an open door to better understanding our partner's pain and discovering the unmet needs behind the hurt.

LISTEN TO THE FLIGHT ATTENDANT

Conflict isn't solved when we run away immediately, withdraw internally, or act defensively. Taking a moment to calm down and chill out keeps us from locking down and moving away from our spouse, creating distance and isolation. Instead, we regain stability and find security as we tamp down anxiety. Scripture reminds us:

> God gave us a spirit not of fear
> but of power and love and self-control.
> 2 TIMOTHY 1:7b ESV

Running to God keeps us from running away from our spouse. Slowing our minds down to calm exaggerated fears keeps us from fleeing, freezing, or escalating the disagreement to unacceptable levels. *God is our flight and fight attendant, and we should listen closely to Him during difficult conversations.* Wisdom is found during a discussion when we ask God in faith for wisdom.

> If any of you lacks wisdom, you should ask God,
> who gives generously to all without finding fault,
> and it will be given to you.
> JAMES 1:5 NIV

Some spouses even ask permission to pray during a quarrel to invite God into the dialogue. Joining hands in unity and bowing heads in spiritual intimacy often dissipates tension and increases connection immediately. I cannot count the number of times in relational conflict when asking someone to pray in the moment led to immediate benefits. The Bible reminds us:

> Let us then approach God's throne of grace with
> confidence, so that we may receive mercy
> and find grace to help in our time of need.
> HEBREWS 4:16 NIV

This may seem redundant when we consider how often we dismiss what an actual flight attendant says in their pre-flight spiel. But when turbulence hits, we quickly recall the previous instructions. Too often, in conflict, we dismiss God's instructions as unnecessary. But unheeded inspiration soon leads to unnecessary instability and intractability in our relationships. We have an in-flight attendant who can guide us through turbulent exchanges. We would be smart to tune in closely. Clarity helps move us toward unity.

LANDING THE PLANE

Nancy and I have different conversational styles, and part of that relates to how our brains are wired, as we covered in a previous chapter. We recently had a phone call about attending our grandson's Christmas play. She proceeded to give a lot of what I considered to be unnecessary details. After all, I'm immersed in writing a book on marital harmony, so I cut in with frustration to ask her to land the plane. My wife gracefully swiveled the dialogue in a better direction. We came to a swift conclusion about when we would leave, rather than crash-landing in a field of irritation.

What I forgot in the moment is that Nancy is a verbal processor who circles the airport before landing somewhere. I have learned that what's happening in her head comes directly from her mouth as she talks it out. Nancy figures out how she's feeling, what she's thinking, and how a decision might work out as she dialogues. The gateway to marital intimacy for Nancy and me is allowing her to unload emotionally and unwind verbally so that she arrives at the conversational runway feeling heard and understood.

Sometimes, this means taking several side trips, pausing at numerous rest stops, and entering various conversational detours to arrive at the intended spot. The key for me is to stay in the conversation and refuse to bail. Many of our fights are over styles of interaction rather than our decisions.

My pattern is much different, and according to neuroscientists, 75% of men process like me. I am an internal processor, so I don't talk it out; instead, I think it through. The beginning of my conversation isn't the start of my thoughts on the matter. In fact, the likelihood is that I've been pondering the matter for a lengthy period and want to find the shortest route to the goal.

Quick questions that Nancy offers when I fire an opening salvo in a dialogue often feel like personal criticism. She isn't aware of how long I've been processing under the surface. I'm hoping she'll see the genius of my logic, quickly nod her head in agreement, and praise the process that brought us to this magical moment. In. My. Dreams.

Yet frequently, her questions throw a wrench in my emotional gears and lead to defensive responses. They bring out my inner Merle Haggard. Challenges and questions mean, "You're walking on the fightin' side of me." This Haggard lyric is a fool's game in Scripture, which says:

> Fools show their annoyance at once,
> but the prudent overlook an insult.
> PROVERBS 12:16 NIV

There are many occasions where my snark derails the discussion because I don't grasp the fact that this is Nancy's first notice of the issue. She is just trying to catch up to where I've already landed.

Her opening questions aren't disparagements, as she is doing externally what I've already done internally. Our goal is to reach the same destination without short-circuiting the process. The key is to engage in these moments without exasperation and process the dialogue in ways consistent with how God made us. I must dial back my tendency to interrupt, edit, summarize, or speed the story along.

Talking through issues allows the knots of tensions to dissolve, emotions to dissipate, and concerns to evaporate. Of course, when time is limited, it's appropriate to ask Nancy to disengage from external processing momentarily, offer a summary statement, and then we can reconsider later.

At other moments, Nancy needs to ask me to act like her girlfriend and process out loud so she can follow what I think and feel. These adjustments facilitate healthy connections that lead to authentic intimacy.

FINDING THE RUNWAY

We've finally arrived where we need to be, on the island's runway of a difficult dialogue. The discussion may entail delivering bad news, making a request, revisiting discussions that went south, or attempting to resolve a persistent problem. Nevertheless, it is time to get down to the nitty-gritty and deal with the issue at hand. We land on the runway and start to address what's going on so we can move forward.

I've spent some time identifying some ways to navigate difficult dialogues, but it does not mean I've mastered them. Initiating a one-on-one works better when I remember where I want to end up—with reconciliation. God gives us the ministry of reconciliation (2 Corinthians 5:18), especially with our spouse. We leave the tarmac and allow a conversation to go sideways when we attack our partner instead of the problem.

Beginning a crucial talk always feels tense as we imagine sirens and signals attempting to call off our conversation. Our mouths go dry, our foreheads glisten, and our thinking skills fly out the window, along with any opening statements we might have crafted. It's never easy to fire up a heart-to-heart that has the potential to get even hotter.

Still, we somehow find the courage to breach the topic and attempt to figure out how to communicate without dancing around the issue or speaking in generalities. We must address the bottom-line questions: "What are we fighting about?" and "What is the cause of our disagreement?" Trouble comes if we refuse to address root causes, avoid the underlying source of the conflict, and do not understand what we are fighting about before we fight. This then leads to dead-end discussions that often shift to other topics. We show up and speak up with clarity as we silence the competing distractions to concentrate on understanding the issue before us.

ASK FOR WHAT YOU WANT

One of the ongoing dialogues in our marriage is about an issue we've dealt with previously: I keep going and going and going! I wake up in the morning as an adrenaline junkie with the switch on full speed ahead. I stay up late, get up early, and survive on a few winks. This. Is. Not. Nancy. Her health issues include fibromyalgia and psoriatic arthritis, which increase her need for downtime, alone moments, sleeping in, and solitude. She loves people and laughs a lot, but she *needs* to decompress. Here's the tension: We often are frustrated with each other because the pace we use in life doesn't match.

I want to do a concert, attend a game, eat with friends, and discover a new hobby all on the same day. Many times, I would drop hints, offer clues, and dance around what I wanted and expect Nancy to know me well enough to figure out my every desire. Regardless of how long we've been married, it's a common refrain with many couples that we don't ask for what we want.

- "Nancy, would you go to the game with me tonight?"
- "Joe, how about we stay at home and watch TV instead of attending that party?"
- "Honey, why don't we take a walk later on?"
- "Hey, babe, I'm feeling a bit lonely. How about a hug?"

The final question arose from interaction with a counselor who, point-blank, told me to ask for what I needed. It was a bit embarrassing but also enlightening to be reminded that I rarely, if ever, just came out and asked for what I wanted. So I've learned, and Nancy has as well, not to use subtle inquiries but to include several reasons you desire a certain resolution. This method works for my three-year-old grandson and for me.

Asking for what you want is the initial opening in a tough conversation, and it should be stated from the opening line. Don't bury the headline in a later paragraph because it feels difficult. Instead, suck it up, buttercup, and dive in headfirst. An *ask* doesn't mean you will get what you want, but you will get absolutely zero of what you never requested. Does the inquiry have the possibility of being hurled up like a clay target and then shot down? Absolutely, but at least your desire is out there, and an immediate rejection doesn't mean it's a hard "no" forever. Don't expect your partner to anticipate what you want without you saying a word. You must ask, even if you've been married for quite a while.

DECIDE HOW YOU'LL DECIDE

When we've ignored a conversation for a lengthy time, it's ludicrous to assume the problem can be solved in one round of talk. Genuine issues unspool over time, and it will take more than a momentary conversation to bring about a resolution. Give each other permission to have a series of discussions, and the pressure will be relieved to get the issue handled in one attempt.

The key is to begin the dialogue; resolution is possible down the road. Talking through an issue starts with a beginning dialogue that entails further conversations at a later date. It is essential to find a time and a place to re-engage that will present an opportunity to grow as we discern and learn.

The reality is that marriage isn't a frequent flier program. We don't accumulate points for a trip to Tahiti because we have logged a ton of marital miles. Tim and Joy Downs wisely stated:

> The greatest mistake that a couple can make
> is to confuse proximity with intimacy.
> Tim and Joy Downs

These are not the same. Marriage makes intimacy possible, but it is not inevitable. Sadly, couples can share a house, bed, and church, be married for years, and be physically close yet miles apart in intimacy. Resolving conflict isn't even the goal—intimacy is the target we are aiming for.

We can use love handles to clean up the messes and repair all the fusses. Love handles are tools to use as we engage one another and learn to have hard conversations and endeavor to fight right. When we understand how to fight the right way, we become a better team and make a bigger difference in our personal spheres of influence. Somehow, we adjust to bring out the best in each other as we endeavor to think the best about each other. We want to end up in the same place together. That's the magic phrase: "We want to do this together." Our greatest fear (Nancy and I) isn't divorce as much as a more sinister enemy—growing increasingly apart and ceasing to do things side by side. How do we become one in marriage?

Marriage thrives when God is unleashed to make two become one flesh (Ephesians 5:31). "Together" is a mutual pursuit of a singular Savior: Jesus Christ. Worship, service, and prayer join our souls at greater depths. Nancy and I are far from perfect, and we are mismatched like every couple on the planet. We stumble and fall time after time, but we've found a way forward to fight the good fight. Engaging in hard conversations is a reminder that we are fighting for each other. Such a fight begins long before a word leaves our mouths.

The fight begins within if we want to win, and we are in this for the long haul. Wheels up, so the wheels don't come off, as we stay in constant connection with Jesus in the cockpit. He wants us to flourish and uses tough conversations to get us there. It's not the route most of us would take voluntarily, but it is the path that leads to real partnership.

Chapter 10

Marriage: The Power of Us

Marriage brings together two individuals who often have distinct perspectives, unique personalities, varied preferences, and different priorities. While the officiant on your wedding day may pronounce the biblical truth that "you are now one" (Mark 10:8), true unity in marriage is not achieved in a single moment but is a process that unfolds over time. The declaration is sudden, but the fulfillment is gradual and ongoing.

THE CHALLENGES OF FAITHFULNESS

As the years pass, remaining faithful to each other and for each other becomes like hugging a porcupine. You know you are supposed to but are not sure it's worth it (if you get my point). It is easy to forget that our responsibility is to fight for one another, rather than against one another. The journey requires pit stops, refueling, and constant check-ins to make sure you are headed to the same landing spot.

REFLECTING ON THE JOURNEY

So, how are things going in your marriage? Perhaps you feel that you are putting in the effort but not seeing the results you had hoped for. You might find yourself stuck in a repetitive routine—doing what is right, caring for children, and managing daily responsibilities—yet notice that the joy and excitement you once anticipated is fading. Physical exhaustion, spiritual depletion, and a sense of hopelessness may set in, leaving you unsure if anything will ever change.

You may begin to suspect the worst about each other, rather than believe the best about each other, and think the coming years will be more of the same, rather than the best is yet to come. Yep. We've been there, done that, got the t-shirt, and brought home the cheap souvenirs. In this type of scenario, a tough talk needs to be scheduled pronto.

NAMING THE REAL ENEMY

Satan is always prowling around (1 Peter 5:8) and looking for a marriage as his afternoon snack. He sees the rough spots you encounter and devises a scheme (Ephesians 6:11) to challenge your biblical vows, sever your marital identity, and offer tempting alternatives to faithfulness. We can choose to flounder in our failures when the enemy takes a bite out of our wedded bliss, or we can stand together in faith to claim the promise of Jesus to step in the gap and fight with us and for us.

Jesus puts every partnership together for a purpose that will push back darkness and shine His light as His will is done and as His Kingdom comes. Too often, we believe the enemy is the person sitting across from us, instead of recognizing the real forces bent on dividing us. We are not opponents; we are on the same team, fighting for "us" against anything that would tear our unity apart.

The enemy of your marriage is not your spouse. The true adversaries are division, bitterness, contempt, and relational drift—the subtle voices and choices that lure you apart. God calls us to unity, not uniformity. Our differences—when united in purpose—can make the duet of our lives a symphony rather than a cacophony.

RECOGNIZE THE REAL ENEMIES THAT DIVIDE US

- **Unresolved Conflict:** Letting minor offenses fester builds walls, not bridges.
- **Bitterness & Unforgiveness:** Bitterness is like drinking poison and expecting the other to get sick. Letting go is for our freedom.
- **Neglect:** When we stop investing time, appreciation, or friendship in our marriage, distance grows, and opportunities for the Enemy increase.
- **Isolation:** The Enemy loves to weaken us through loneliness, shame, or silence. Unity is built when we refuse to withdraw or stonewall each other.

FIGHTING FOR US: THE ESSENTIALS

We care about the essentials because going back to the basics, spending time individually and in community, and reminding each other of our initial vows are lifesavers in our relationship. It's not grand promises that build a strong marriage, but small incremental changes and choices in rhythms, routines, habits, and postures that make a marriage.

1. Choose Each Other Daily

- Love is a decision. The real fight is to keep saying yes to your spouse, even when feelings fade or when it's hard.

- Begin and end every day with a gesture of connection—a kiss, a prayer, a word of encouragement.

2. Name and Tame What Divides

- Identify persistent issues and confront them together, not as adversaries but as allies.
- Practice gentle start-ups; refuse escalating blame or contempt. Remember, your spouse is not the problem—division is.

3. Forgive as You Have Been Forgiven

- Forgiveness is the ladder out of the pit. Grieve, gain perspective, choose to forgive, and repeat until it takes. Do not climb down into bitterness. Forgiveness is not a one-and-done, but a process that keeps us climbing toward unity.

4. Make Peacemaking Pursuits

- Peacemaking is not keeping the peace by avoiding hard things; it's moving toward your spouse, taking the risk of vulnerability, and facing issues together.
- When conflict comes, pause to ask: "Are we fighting each other, or fighting for each other?"

5. Cultivate "Us" Rituals

- **Cultivate small daily connections.** Create rituals—hellos, goodbyes, inside jokes, date nights, regular check-ins—moments that weave a safety net under the marriage.
- **Bond face-to-face.** Commit to 15 minutes a day with conversation. It may happen as you are doing other daily tasks. Share wins and grins as well as frowns and clowns (You

can figure this one out). We make time for each other, so we don't end up missing out on each other's lives.
- **Plan date times**. Schedule it well in advance and plan for a couple of hours. This isn't carpooling or activities for kids. It's *we*-time planned exclusively for you. It doesn't need to be expensive or complicated, but it does need to be intentional.
- **Schedule sex**. Yep, put it on the calendar. It's more prone to happen and less likely to be interrupted if you use a code word and use a Sharpie to put it in the blocks on the calendar. Plus, the lower desire spouse can mentally gear up for what's coming around the corner.
- **Yearly Getaways** – Advance the romance. Sometimes it was a 'staycation' and other times it was a long week with coordination of the budget and childcare. We discovered that a marriage in tune led to a family walking in harmony.
- **Celebrate wins and withstand losses as a team**. Make *we* matter more than *me*. Discuss what is right, wrong, confusing, and missing in your marriage. We do this as a church staff, but we also incorporate it into the inventories of our marriages.

INVESTMENT NOT INTENTION

God's dream for marriage is an intimate partnership, not disconnected roommates or resigned survivors. The goal isn't avoiding conflict but learning tools for repair and reconnection. All the best intentions never get you to your destination: a flourishing marriage. Marriages thrive on the principle of compounding: daily investments of time, intentionality, and empathy bring a return far beyond what you could ever imagine. The routines, rituals, rhythms, and rest you invest will make your and God's dreams come to fruition. Don't stop fighting as if the battle is over. As you fight for your marriage together:

- Pray for God's protection over your unity.
- Invite God into your divides—He is the master artisan who turns messes into masterpieces.
- Cheer each other on toward becoming all God intended.

Most clashes are not communication failures but lapses of preparation. Instead of waiting for turbulence to bring up a subject, start at the gate. Every conflict is a fight, and the goal is not to circle the runway or crash in chaos but to land together. Arrival includes reducing speed and committing to a plan. Wheels down means clarifying plans, owning your part, and deciding on how to create verbal parachutes. The goal of every tough talk is not being right but staying together.

The greatest testimony of your marriage will not be that you never struggled, but that you never quit fighting. Persevere in the marathon; keep running till the finish line, hand in hand. Your unity will not only heal your home but will be a beacon to others longing for hope.

Stay side by side, back-to-back, united, surrendered, and ready to overcome anything that divides.

Fight for "us." Because "us" is worth fighting for.

About the Author

Dr. Joe R. Stewart has been serving God in vocational pastoral ministry since 1988. He currently serves as the lead pastor of First Baptist Church of Seminole, Texas. He and his wife of 45 years have a passion for strengthening marriages and encouraging pastors throughout the United States and the world.

Joe earned his Doctor of Education from Southern Baptist Theological Seminary in Louisville, KY, complete with a full-length dissertation. He is also a certified "Together in Texas" premarital counselor and trained as a Prepare and Enrich facilitator, along with accreditation as a SYMBIS instructor. He has served on multiple ministry boards as a member and as a chairperson. Nancy serves as a grief and loss encouragement facilitator in her church.

As a writer, Joe hopes to give practical and inspirational advice to couples and premarital couples. Combining personal experience, pastoral seasoning, and biblical wisdom, his goal is to support couples during difficult moments in their relationships.

Joe and Nancy have ministered to couples and pastors, and wives in Pakistan, Ukraine, Mexico, Portugal, and Spain, and to underground pastors and wives brought into Armenia. They serve as marital instructors in *Three2One Marriage* conferences held across the United States.

The Stewarts have three daughters: Pamela, Kimberly (Bryan), and Kristen (Chris). They cherish their seven grandsons: Joey, Christopher, Bryce, Brayden, Brody, Luke, and Hudson.

To contact the author of this book:
    Joe Stewart
    www.fromthisdayforward.net
    joerstewart@gmail.com